Pioneers of the Ozarks

Pioneers of the Ozarks

By

LENNIS L. BROADFOOT

ILLUSTRATED BY THE AUTHOR

The CAXTON PRINTERS, Ltd.
CALDWELL, IDAHO
1944

COPYRIGHT 1944 BY
THE CAXTON PRINTERS, LTD.
CALDWELL, IDAHO

457233

M 12 18 44

Dedication

In memory of my pleasant contacts with these people, and for their kind and courteous co-operation with me in procuring this valued collection of art, I am hereby expressing my appreciation and good will by dedicating this book to the "pioneer fathers and mothers" of the Missouri hills.

Preface

It may be of interest to the reader, before looking over the contents of this book, to know something about how this volume of work was procured, how done, for what purpose, etc. Therefore, permit me, as the "artist and author," to make the introduction with a few preliminary remarks.

First, I wish to assure you that each and every picture contained in this book has been drawn or painted by hand, and directly from life sittings, except one picture—"An Old Water Mill," which is a mental or memory picture—and that no photographs have been used.

Second, the medium used in this work was charcoal, except in the few landscapes, which were done in oil. The pictures were procured through contacts that I made with the people in and around their homes, as I have trudged throughout the Missouri Hills.

The short stories are such as fell from the lips of the sitters, as I was busily engaged drawing their portraits, and have been written in their own native dialect.

They are the true native types, and people that I know intimately. Every picture is a careful life study. I have treated them seriously, honestly, literally, and without injecting a vestige of satire.

Third, the purpose of this volume of work is to preserve a true picture record of the pioneers of the hills, their strange customs of living that are so rapidly vanishing, and a life that is so different from anything known to modern folk, that it should be educational, especially to the younger generation who know nothing of the joys and hardships of primitive ways.

For some of these drawings it was necessary for me to carry my easel and drawing material, and walk from one to one and one-fourth mile to find my subjects deep in a canyon, or high up on a peak, where it was impossible to drive a car.

Lennis Leonard Broadfoot

7

Table of Contents

TABLE OF CONTENTS — Continued

10

Pioneers of the Ozarks

Lennis Leonard Broadfoot

Dear Reader:

I am sure that the first question to enter your mind, upon opening the covers of this volume of work, will be, "Who is the author, is he a native, and of what nationality?"

At this point, and as a means of introducing myself as the artist, author, and sole originator of this book, I shall endeavor to give you some facts in a brief story concerning my life as a native of the Missouri hills, how I started out to become an artist, that culminated in my present profession, and such work as this volume contains.

It is only a simple story of a lad who is part Cherokee Indian, as the name "Broadfoot" readily suggests, whose parents came to Missouri from the smoky mountains of Tennessee early in their lives, and later in years homesteaded a forty-acre tract of government land high up on a hill in north Shannon County near Eminence, Missouri, along the wild and rugged Current River, when it was only a wilderness of heavy timber and underbrush. Here they erected a small log cabin with a stone chimney, and began the work of clearing off the timber and making the little farm.

It was in this small log hut on the old homestead that I was born, and where I spent the first six or seven years of my life, being lambasted and kicked because I kept the walls and windowpanes of this quaint old shack littered with my crude sketches that I called "art," and which was the true outcropping of my art career.

My father, James Henderson Broadfoot, who was a quarter Cherokee Indian, but who possessed all the qualities and characteristics of a full blood, seemed to pick about the highest spot he could find in the Ozarks, upon which to establish a home. It was more like an "observation tower," but a very beautiful and picturesque location.

From the doorway of our old cabin home we could see far away into the blue haze of the Ozark hills. We could hear the sound of bells, worn by range stock, and could see horses and cattle grazing on the wild free range, on green, grassy glades far in the distance.

We were about the first in the neighborhood to catch the glitter of the early morning sunrise, and the last to be penetrated by its rays as it sank in the Western skies.

It was here that we could lie in bed at night and listen to the song of the whippoorwill and the nightingale, as they sat upon the clapboard roof of our tiny shack, and could hear the wolves howl, and the call of the hunter's horn far away, as the hound-dogs chased the fox on the hills all around our house.

It was all about the premises and surroundings of this old homestead that I loitered in my early childhood life, just a ragged, tattered, barefoot lad. I was quite rude, did about everything, except what my parents wanted me to do, and possessed the traits of an Indian to the extent that I carried a bow and arrow with me wherever I went, and a pocketfull of chalk, paper, and pieces of lead pencils, or anything else I could use to sketch pictures.

I slipped and sneaked here and there about the place, secreting myself in clumps of brush, under cliffs of rock, behind logs and stumps, or even in the field, where I would hide in shocks of corn, seeking a chance to shoot something with my bow and arrow, or sketch a picture.

Slowly and quietly I crept around the barn, and with my bow and arrow shot and killed

13

Picture in Center:

"L.S. Broadfoot," a self portrait, drawn by the use of a mirror. The above picture, is my birth place, a small tract of government land which my father, "J.H.Broadfoot" homesteaded in the year of 1891 when it was only a wild forest of heavy timber, and on which he erected a log cabin with stone chimney. This is located high upon a hill near by a small winding stream known as "Barren Fork," near Current River, in Shannon Co.Mo Lower left; is a little box school-house near by our homestead, where I entered school, and lower right, is my church house, Known as "the old log Church".

14

rats and mice through the cracks of the old log corncrib. Then away I went to where I shot and killed chipmunks as they scampered along the rail fence that enclosed our farm, and then back to the house, where I would sneak around and try my luck on the cats, dogs, and even on my mother's frying chickens; and this is where I usually wound up in serious trouble, and paid a dear price for all my sport and fun.

I always liked to go to school, because it was a splendid place for "character study," and a grand opportunity to refill my pockets with chalk, pieces of pencils and things, to use in my crude sketches on the walls and windowpanes at home; however, it was not too healthy to be caught drawing pictures in school, as I was many times, and paid the penalty by going up to the front, drawing a circle on the blackboard, and standing on my tiptoes with my nose in the circle for a long time, as punishment for my artistic ability.

My mother made me go to church and Sunday school quite frequently, though I did not like that so much, and often protested, but to no avail; and many times I did not get started on my way until after I had received a few lashes around the seat of my pants with a strap of leather or a branch that my mother had broken from a peach tree.

Our little community church, built of logs, stood about three-fourths of a mile down the valley from our homestead, and since I was compelled to go, I usually made the best of it, and went fully equipped to do what I could in sketching pictures of hill characters that dropped in from here and there; and especially our pastor, Joe Thompson, whom we called "Uncle Joe." He was tall and lank, and with long white whiskers that brushed his stomach, he would stand straight in the pulpit and preach a sermon of great length, giving me plenty of time to study and practice as I sat quietly crouched in one corner of the little log church.

In my natural desire to become an artist, I have since early in my childhood days, made character study a specialty.

I used to sit by our hearthstone in our old log cabin home, when only a small tot, and attempt to sketch pictures of the pioneer mothers and fathers of the hills as they came in and sat before our fireplace to smoke their clay pipes, chew their tobacco and spit, talk of the Civil War days, and tell stories of how they came to Missouri from the hills of Tennessee, Kentucky, Alabama, Virginia, and elsewhere in the East, in ox wagons, being many weeks on the road.

These were the folk that I enjoyed and who told the stories that I liked to hear, and as they talked, I made careful studies of them and tried very hard to get a picture, though very crude of course, but when it was over and they went away, I had some sort of a picture that I had made either with a cheap lead pencil on paper, a white chalk sketch on the wall or a slate, or with a piece of soap on the windowpane.

It was in those days that it occurred to me that some day, I would become a finished professional artist, and make a history in portraits of the pioneer settlers of the hills.

With this ambition and thought in mind, I went on in my persistent practice of studying and sketching from life, sketching characters wherever I found them, with no one to encourage me; rather, it seemed that everyone wished to discourage me with the comment, "Oh, you'll never make it," or, "you cain't do no good at that." Still I refused to accept such advice, for I felt that with all the fun I was having in sketching hill characters here and there, I had a treasure of wealth in happiness, regardless of money.

My mother passed away while I was still in my teens, soon after which I decided to go West, to acquire a broader perspective by sketching pictures of cowboys and Indians. Like other artists of the "Regional School," I had this to do before I could appreciate picturesque subjects near at hand. For many years I roamed through the Western states from the Canadian border to San Diego, California, a part of which time I worked as a ranch hand, and in Montana, where I spent five years, and made studies and sketches of cowboys and Indians.

During my years of roaming I took up the study of art with the Federal School, Inc., Minneapolis, Minn., and graduated.

For a while I worked in the field of commercial art, making drawings for advertising purposes, but I have always been a "free lancer" and have never tied myself down to working for others; and never at any time did I give up character study and sketching, always thinking of the wonderful studies back home, and my childhood plans to do them some day.

My portraits, both in oil and charcoal, can be seen in many homes and public places throughout the country.

My later days in the West were spent in southern California, where I drew many portraits, and from where I left, when I came to Missouri in November, 1936, and began drawing the series of pioneer settlers of the hills, which I have on hand at this time, and which is a culmination of my dreams of childhood days.

And now after all of my experience in portraiture and studies from life here, there, and elsewhere, I have come to the conclusion that I would rather draw a picture of an Ozark grandmother loitering around her cabin home with a pipe in her mouth, than all the glamour girls in Hollywood.

LENNIS LEONARD BROADFOOT

October 1, 1941

Salem, Missouri.

Pioneers of the Ozarks

Nancy Caroline Moser

Crocker, Pulaski County, Missouri

Mrs. Moser Says:

"I was born in Pulaski County, Mo., March 27, 1848. I am ninety-two years old.

"I was twelve years old when the Civil War started, and my father had to go and was killed, and left mother and a big family of us children, and oh! what a time we had gettin' through!

"I have always lived in the hills of Pulaski County and don't know nothin' about other places, and I never traveled none, 'cause I have always had my nose held right down to the grindin' stone to make a livin' for the family.

"I never got to go to school none, and all the larnin' I got was jist what my mother larned me. We had an old blue-back spellin' book an' she would set down late at night after we got through with our work sich as cardin' wool, spinnin', knittin', weavin' carpets, and hullin' beans, and call me up to her, and give me lessons out of this old spellin' book, by the light of the old tallow candlestick.

"She kept this up till she larned me jist enough to know how to read a little, and as soon as we was able, we bought us a coal oil lamp, and I thought they was the finest thing and give the brightest light of anything I ever see'd. So I kept on studyin' and larnin' till I got so I could read the Bible, and that's about all I've read in my life, and nothin' gives me so much contentment and pleasure as to set down by the light of my old coal oil lamp after my day's work is done, and read my Bible.

"I don't care nothin' about readin' these old newspapers 'cause you cain't tell whether it's the truth or not, and after you have read it all through, you know a whole lot less than you did when you started.

"Give me my Bible, my coal oil lamp and pipe, and you can have your electric lights, cigarettes, and newspapers."

18

Julius Hulsey

The Ozark Fox Hunter

Mr. Julius Hulsey of Dent County, Mo., is seen here on his mule with his gun strapped to his saddle, blowing his horn as his dogs leap and bark, eager to start on their early morning fox chase. He says:

"There's nothin' on earth that gives me the thrill, pep an' vigor, as to get up at three-thirty in the cool October mornin's, jump on Ol' Jack, give my horn a toot, an' see ol' Drum an' Blue rare and fonch as we start out into the hills on a fox chase.

"The sound of this ol' horn railly sets 'em wild, an' puts 'em goin', an' I think Ol' Jack understands it about as well as Ol' Drum or Blue does, 'cause I have sat on his back many a cool, frosty mornin' long before daybreak, high upon these Ozark mountain peaks an' listened to Ol' Drum an' Blue after they had jumped the fox way down in the holler below me, an' chased it back over the high divides, an' so far away I could no longer hear 'em, then circle back, close to where they first started, and again vanish clear out of my hearin', an' I would sit and listen, an' wait fer hours, 'till finally I would take a notion to call 'em in, when I would rare up in my saddle an' sound this ol' horn so loud, Ol' Jack would flop his ears an' drop his tail; but many times Ol' Drum an' Blue would be miles away an' couldn't hear it, an' would have to go in without 'em, an' maybe it would be three or four days before they made it home, an' would be so sore an' stiff they could hardly walk for a few days.

"This wuz usually the case if it wuz a red fox chase, but if it happened to be a gray fox, they either caught it purty soon, or made it take a hole. Red foxes air long winded an' can run longer an' faster than a gray fox can.

"Fox chasin' is the greatest an' oldest outdoor sport known to pioneer hill dwellers. We ol'-timers get together in great numbers, an' each feller has a pack ov houn's an' all go out on a "wolf drive" or a "fox chase," an' have the greatest time ye ever se'ed; an' finally we organized a fox hunter's association, where the people of different counties joined in membership, an' all got together annually fer a week's fox chase, then our membership increased until we now have what is known as the National Fox Hunter's Association whereby the fox hunters from nearly every state in the union get together each year, with their houn'-dogs; an' say, what a happy get-to-gether this is!

"In October, 1940, the State Fox Hunters' Meet was held in Salem, Mo., where about 475 houn'-dogs wuz brought in frum all parts of the U. S., an' when all these dogs wuz scattered through the hills, say, did we have music. An' to people who don't know, an' have never had experience in this sort of Ozark life, ye don't know what ye air missin'."

John Musgrave

Veteran of the U. S. Civil War

Mr. Musgrave, who was very feeble at the time this picture was drawn, says:

"I am a soldier of the Civil War. I fought in the Northern army. I am ninety-seven years old and don't feel like talkin', and I can't remember much anymore, 'cause my mind is bad.

"I was shot up and hurt awful bad while in the army, but I've lived a long time anyway. It's hard to kill a good man, but there was many times while in the army, that I thought I'd starve to death. Oh, what a struggle it was! We won freedom for the colored race, but I thought we'd never get the Southerners whipped.

"I know all the hardships of dreadful wars. I can't remember dates, and would like to tell you all about the Civil War, but I'm too feeble. There's one thing I can remember and that is what an awful time we had to make a livin' when we come back home.

"It was just another struggle, or war of starvation. How on earth can a man live for ninety-seven years, after he has been starved, beat up, and shot up like I've been?

"But that's all that wars are good for, and still we have them, but for my part, I say, 'God deliver us from all wars, and bring peace among men!' "

L L Broadfoot

Katherine Burk

Timber, Missouri

MRS. BURK SAYS:

"I am one hundred an' eleven years ol', an' wuz born an' raised in the Ozark hills, an' don't know nothin' else.

"I wuz born February 13, 1829. I guess I am about the oldest person in these hills.

"I have smoked an' chawed terbacker ever since I wuz a little girl, an' I don't believe terbacker hurts a body either, if they use it right, but the way young people use it now-days, I think it hurts 'em. They sit around, suckin' cigarettes an draw the smoke down in their lungs, an' soon they get to coughin' an' wheezin' in their lungs like a pig that's sick with cholera, an' their health is gone an' they die young.

"My pappy an' mammy smoked an' chawed too, but they smoked a clay pipe like I do, an' we never smoked or chawed nothin' only what we raised ourselves.

"I reckon I'm ol'-fashioned an' foagy, but I believe the ol' way of life is best.

"I believe in moon signs, witches, an' all them things. People used to think I wuz a witch. Lots of people don't know what a witch is.

"If you don't know, I'll tell ye: A witch is an ol' person—usually a womern, with humpback, an' goosenecked with long chin an' nose, with stringy, frizzlie hair, deep wrinkles in her face, an' her eyes as glassy an' glairy as a dyin' calf's eye, an' sets aroun' or snoops aroun' an' says nothin' to nobody, an' has the power to send their spirit away to work around the homes of others an' do things.

"The reason why they won't talk is 'cause their mind an' spirit is allers away some-wheres else. An' ye cain't become a witch or have the power of witchcraft till ye air at least seventy years ol'.

"I can recognize every witch as soon as I look at 'em. They can shore do ye a lot of torment. We have had 'em to come to our home in the night an tie knots in our hosses' an' cows' tails, an' pick all the feathers out of our ol' gray rooster's tail an' sich things as that, an' here's what we done to stop it, or kill the spirit:

"The witch usually has a rabbit to carry her spirit here an' there, doin' devilment, an' we watched our chance to shoot an' kill the rabbit, or if we didn't kill the rabbit, we would keep our minds good an' strong on the person we thought wuz the witch while we stuck a dishrag full of pins an' throw it in the fire an' burn it, or take a ball of yarn an' pierce it with a darnin' needle with our minds concentrated on that certain ol' witch.

"We would get 'em that way."

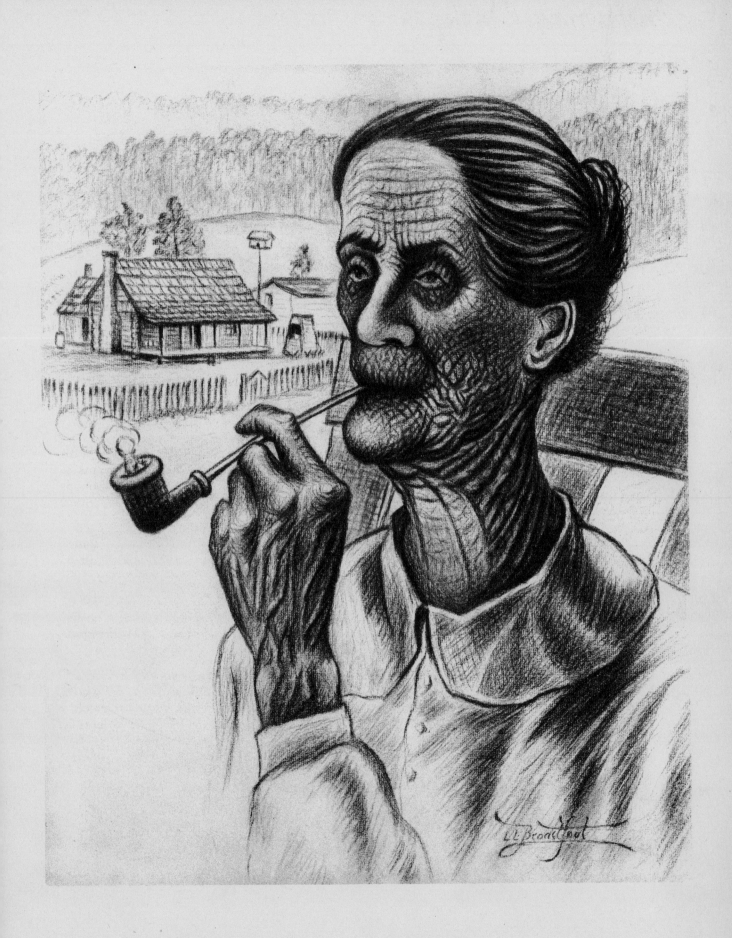

The Soap Maker

This picture was drawn by the artist and writer, away down in the hills on Barren Fork of Current River, near Timber, Missouri.

It is of an Ozark grandmother who is busily engaged in making soap by hand around the old dilapidated log home.

This is the old-fashioned "hopper and kettle process," whereby wood ashes are carried from the fireplace in the home and dumped into the "V" shaped ash hopper seen in the foreground, which also sets in a "V" shaped trough.

When the hopper is nearly filled with ashes, water is carried and poured in, which filters down through the ashes and comes out a red liquid lye. This lye is then poured into a kettle that contains bones and meat scraps, and under which a slow, smoldering fire is kept burning while grandma stirs and cooks it as the lye eats and dissolves the bones and scraps into a hard soap, some of which may be seen lying on the table. Through this process, they are able to make either hard or soft soap.

When "butcher day" comes for the Ozark farmer, the housewife is usually the busiest member of the family, and has more work to do than anyone else, as she goes about taking care of meat scraps, grinding them into sausage, and salvaging other fragments and bones, by setting them away in baskets and boxes in the smokehouse, to wait for soap-making day to come.

As one travels through the Ozark hills, it is very common to see the mother beside the log cabin home, bent over the washboard and tub, putting out the family wash by hand, or standing over a large kettle stirring soap, while the barefoot lad comes trekking down the hillside carrying wood in his arms, to keep the fire going under the kettle.

They usually make their soap during the dark of the moon, as they say it gets much firmer and better. If made in the light of the moon, that is, during the time of moonlit nights, then the soap is unfirm, light, and fluffy, and not so good.

Wash-Day in the Ozarks

This is a wash-day scene on what is known as the old "Potts farm" down in the Ozark hills near Hardage, Mo.

This log house, one of the oldest in southeast Missouri, was built prior to Civil War days. Thousands of pounds of bacon have been cured, and thousands of pounds of pumpkins and apples have been dried, hanging to the rafters in the attic of this pioneer hut.

On the outside walls there is usually to be seen hanging the old hand washboard and wash tub, crosscut saws, cowbells, steel traps, and wild animal peltry stretched on boards and hung on the walls around the old stone chimney to dry for the market, such as raccoon, opossum, skunk, weasel, muskrat, and wild mountain bobcat skins.

The few acres of farmland of this quaint old home are enclosed with old-fashioned rail fence which is densely wrapped in wild grape vines, and around which stands a mass of brush and timber, such as sumac, hazelnut, hickory nut, white walnut, black walnut, buckeye, and oak trees.

One can stand in the door of this log cabin home and shoot squirrels from the tops of the tall hickory nut trees, and see them scampering and playing among the grapevines along the old rail fence. The house sets back upon a hillside, far back up a deep narrow canyon running up from Sinkin Creek, all around which can be seen high mountain peaks.

You will notice from the clothes that hang on the line tied to the walnut tree, that it was a breezy day when the washing was put out. Wood was carried down from the hillside and burned under the kettle to boil the clothes. Near by is the old hand-dug well, that's walled with rock, from which the water is drawn up with a rope and pulley.

Friday is wash day in the Ozarks, and the ironing is done on Saturday for clean clothes on Sunday morning.

John Henry Smith

Gladden, Missouri

JOHN SAYS:

"You can find fellers all down through the Ozarks here that can do jist about anything ye can think ov, anywhere frum ox trainers and drivers, to locomotive engineers, pilots, an' electricians.

"Some ov us may look sorta tough an' weatherbeaten, but when it comes to the test, we know a few things an' can railly turn the trick an' do things.

"Ov course, I'm jist an ol' ox trainer myself, but I claim to know how to do that, an' do it well. I wuz born and raised in these ol' hills an' have handled 'em all my life, an' when I break a yoke ov oxen an' train 'em up to work, they know what it's all about, an' a womern can purtnye take 'em an plow onions with 'em—yes, or your grandma can handle 'em, plow 'em, ride 'em, milk 'em, or do anything with 'em, 'cause I can take this ol' whip an' jist play a tune around their tails, noses, and ears, an' they railly toe the mark, an' dance to the music, an' when I'm all through with 'em, ye can jist talk to 'em like talkin' to a man, an' they'll mind ye.

"I never see'd a pair ov dad-burned oxen that I couldn't handle, an' if they air trained right, they air the most obedient critter on earth.

"My pappy used to work 'em an' showed me how to do it, an' I won a cash prize one time in an ox drivin' contest.

"There hain't many oxen to be see'd any more these days, 'cause Henry Ford come along with that ol' road louse of his an' put 'em clear out ov business till ye cain't hardly find nairy one, an' put everybody on the hog.

"Dad-burn the luck anyway! I wonder what things air comin' to. I druther ride an ox an' peddle homemade soap fer a livin', than to see things in the mess they air in today, an' still, they call it modern, but it railly looks like 'vegetable soup' to me, an' if our givernment was usin' oxen today instead of air planes, our boys wouldn't be so apt to have to go over an' settle ol' European troubles again; but no, ye can never tell jist what's waitin' fer ye around the corner, an' I wonder what it will be in twenty years frum now."

34

L.J. Broadfoot

Logging in the Ozarks

These sturdy oxen, Bob and Ball, are owned by Mr. Dal Clayton of Licking, Mo., in Texas County.

Mr. Clayton states that "they are ten years old, weigh about fourteen hundred pounds each, and have farmed and hauled logs and lumber since they were three years old."

This picture was drawn from life, as the artist found Bob and Ball hitched to the old log wagon. In order to demonstrate to the artist the obedience of the well-trained oxen, Mr. Clayton took them loose from the wagon and lead them away a distance of about two hundred feet to where he left them standing, then, walking back to the wagon alone, Mr. Clayton picked up the wagon tongue and yoke, and gave the command, "Come here, Bob!" and Bob very obediently walked around to his place and put his neck in the yoke. Then came another command, "Come here, Ball!" Ball was not so quick to obey, when suddenly came the cry, "Get around here!" Then Ball scampered hurriedly around to where he took his place in the yoke by his work mate Bob.

These oxen are well-trained to their duties on the farm as well as in the woods, and since they were three years old have been working on the farm during the summer, cultivating crops and making hay, then in the fall they are taken to the woods where they haul logs to the mill, and lumber to the market.

They are used in the hills where trucks cannot be driven, and are especially good for skidding logs from deep, rugged canyons and steep mountainsides, where it is quite impossible to use vehicles of any kind.

The oxen is also very effective and useful in low marsh lands, and can draw great loads where horses and mules cannot be used at all. Bob and Ball are the power kings of the Texas County hills, and with this old wagon loaded down with large green pine and oak logs, they have plowed out deep ruts in the steep, rough Ozark mountainsides in places that seem quite inaccessible, and where these old wheel ruts will be seen for years hence.

Mr. Clayton says, "I think lots of Bob and Ball and could get a fancy price for 'em, but I don't want to sell 'em."

They are very beautiful animals, both in form and color—a deep red, with white faces.

L.L. Broadfoot

Outlet from "Round Spring" at State Park
Shannon County Mo. Highway No 19

Outlet to Round Spring

This is the outlet to the tunnel through which the waters flow from Round Spring, a distance of two hundred feet away. The original picture from which this was taken is also a large canvas painting.

Round Spring

This is a picture of Round Spring in the Missouri State Park, at Round Spring, Missouri. The original from which this photostatic copy was made is a large canvas painting which was done by the artist and author of this book.

This beautiful round spring of crystal clear water forms a natural bowl, and is deeply set in the mountainside, fourteen miles north of Eminence, Missouri, in Shannon County.

It is about seventy feet in diameter, almost perfectly round, and is about 125 feet deep, with a flowing capacity of approximately 101,600,000 gallons daily. Its waters flow quietly through the natural tunnel for about two hundred feet to where it comes out, and rapidly races away to a distance of about four hundred feet further to where it empties into Current River.

Thousands of tourists visit and camp around this spring every year.

39

Chester Piatt

"The Ozark Root Digger"

Round Spring, Missouri

CHESTER SAYS:

"I guess it's perfectly natural fer us fellers that live down in the hills to brag about what the Ozarks air good fer, an' I guess it's mostly cause most ov us wuz born an' raised here, an' hain't never been nowhere an' don't know no better, but railly, these ol' Missouri hills produce a thousand and one things that air a benefit to the human race, that the average person don't know about.

"Look in this sack I've got here! What is it, an' what's it good fer? Well, it's May apple roots, an' they're used in makin' medicines—herb tonics, pills, an' other kinds ov medicines—an' we not only have the May apple, but there's the yaller root—or Golden Seal some people call it—an' the red pecoon, the ginseng, the skull cap, the life everlasting, the sassafras, an' lots others I could mention, that air used and made into medicines, an' all this grows right around my house here in the Current River hills, an' that's the way I make my extra money to buy a little terbacker, coffee, sugar, salt, an' other necessities for the family.

"I've got a little stumpy, rocky farm an' a big family, an' we have purty lean years when we don't raise much crop, an' money is tight, so I take my little hand pick an' go out in the river bottoms an' dig roots, an' spread 'em out on the house roof, dry 'em in the sun, an' sell 'em.

"The May apple, red pecoon, an' sassafras, an' roots like that, bring about three cents a pound when dried, an' a good strong man that knows how to dig 'em can dig twenty-five pounds a day—that is, twenty-five pounds ov dried roots.

"We've got fellers here in these hills that hain't done nairy thing in their lives fer a livin', only dig roots in the summer an' set traps an' catch varments in the winter; an' I can usually tell who they air, the first time I see 'em, without askin' 'em what they do fer a livin'.

"They generly have long hair that comes clear down around their years, an' about an eight-weeks' groth ov beard, an' with lots ov hair on their chests, their mouthes twisted a little to one side, wearin' a flapped down hat, an' ol' run-over shoes, with a patch or two on the seat ov their pants; an' when you see one like that, you can jist bet yer false teeth that he don't do nairy thing in this world only dig roots an' trap fer a livin'.

"A feller can work at about anything he wants to, to make a livin' here in the Ozarks. He can be a root digger, a fisherman, a hunter, or work in the timber an' be a tie maker, a basket maker, a lumberjack, or chair maker; he can be a farmer, or if he wants to be a miner, he can go to Saint Francis County, Mo., where the biggest lead mines in the world air runnin' full blast, an' get a job; so what about the Ozarks?"

Henry Gove

Osage County, Missouri

MR. GOVE SAYS:

"You can say what you dad-burn please about cheap transportation an' the best ways to get around through the Ozark hills, but give me the ol' jinney. They've got 'em all beat, an' it don't cost nothin' to feed 'em. This ol' jinney ov mine lives on sassafras an persimmon brush.

"They're the finest thing to ride I ever see'd, an' can go anywhere over all kinds ov mountains an' climb around ledge rocks, an' can purtnye climb a tree.

"I live a long ways frum town an' I'm eighty-four years ol' an' live alone, an' I don't know what I'de do if it wuzn't fer my jinney an' dog. I have to go to town once in a great while an' get a load ov groceries.

"Sometimes I get up jist at daybreak, saddle my ol' jinney, an' take my dog an' gun, an' go deep back in the hills an' stay all day long, an' many times I ride fur back up to the highest peak I can find late in the evening to see the beautiful sunset over the Ozark divide. God never made anything purtier than an Ozark sunset.

"I draw the ol' age pension 'cause I'm too ol' to work, so I put in about all ov my time ridin' my jinney through the hills sight-seein'. When I go out to stay all day, I allers take a few nubbins ov corn along to feed my jinney, an' a lunch fer myself an' dog, an' go to a nice cold spring where we can get a good drink, an' there we take a good rest, an' I often lay down an' sleep till my jinney eats brush a while. Sometimes my ol' dog wakes me up, barkin' up on the hill when he's got a squirrel treed, an' I go up an shoot the squirrel out an' take it home to eat.

"I live in a little log cabin, an' hain't got no womern, so my dog an' jinney is all I got to keep me company, but we make the best ov it, an' have a purty good time."

43

Miller Bell

Iron County, Missouri

Mr. Bell Says:

"I am seventy-five years ol' an' was born an' raised in the Iron County hills, an' have worked at this, that, an' t'other all my life, till I am broke down an' hain't no good any more, an' now all I can do is jist plod around with this ol' 'walkin' cane' an' see what others air doin', an' hear 'em talk.

"I usually come to town on Saturday if I can get here, an' after I plod around on the streets fer a while, shakin' hands with ol' timers, an' findin' out if their folks air all well, an' how the crops air, I go into a grocer store an' sit down on a sack ov taters or a sack ov shorts or a goods' box, an' hear 'em talk about how to run the givernment.

"Now I hain't no idea much how to run this givernment, an' don't claim to be so dad-burn smart, but I know there's a screw loose somewhere! I live on a little patch ov land an' have allers been a little one-horse farmer, raisin' a few pigs an' calves down here in the hills, an' have jist worked my hocks off, an' still somebody else got it! An' who wuz it, the packers, or the merchant?

"Why gee whizz! us fellers can raise a hog an' ship it to St. Louis, an' not even get enough out ov it to pay the freight ov the dad-burn thing, an' sometimes haft to send a basket ov eggs along to help pay the freight; an' the packers will take that durned hog, an' butcher it, an' save everything, hoof, hair, an' all, an' even bottle up the squeal an' sell it fer more than we get fer the whole hog!

"Now I think the givernment ort to look into things like that, take the whole works apart an' fix the loose wheels. Course, ye can allers get plenty ov goods' box an' tater sack advice around the little grocer store, ov how to run the givernment, but now actually, fellers, there's shore a magget in the apple somewhere, 'cause us fellers don't get enough money for a three-year-ol' steer when we ship it out to buy enough ov it's taller to grease a shot gun barrel after it makes the round an' comes back to our small town butcher!

"Sometimes I think I could set on a sack ov shorts, or sack ov taters, an' run a better givernment than some ov 'em do. These duck-billed, beer-bellied politicians, come around at election time, makin' their soap-box speeches, an' tellin' us ol' humpy farmers how they're goin' to take the whole works apart an' see what makes it tick, an' they're goin' to put in a new cogwheel an' make it free wheelin' fer us fellers, but ever' time one ov these greasy tongued liars puts in a new wheel, it's one that grinds a new kink in our legs, an' a hump on our backs.

"I've been comin' to town fer a long time an' talkin' it over with these fellers an' we hain't never got it fixed yet, an' I can see that if we ever get anywhere, we've got to do somethin' besides set on a sack ov taters an' talk; 'cause things air gettin' in a mess, an' taxes goin' higher'n a giraff's back, an' all ye can hear is, "Revenue! revenue! revenue!" an' the first thing ye know, ye'll haf to wear a revenue stamp on the seat ov yer pants to have the right to set down.

"I've hearn so much talk an' had so many promises I'm fed up an' disgusted; an' I've worked my life away, an' all I've got to show fer it, is this ol' walkin' cane, an' a hump on my back like a camel. I reckon us ol' farmers air about the only animal on earth that can stand more than one skinnin', an' we git it, ever time we vote, or sell a pig."

44

COPE AND CO. GROCERIES.

100 LBS.
PEACOCK
KANSAS WHE
GREY SHORTS

L.J. Broadfoot

45

Arminta Taylor

Age 91

Gladden, Missouri

MRS. TAYLOR STATES:

"I have lived on this ol' farm sixty-five years, and have raised a family of eleven children.

"My husband was a soldier during the Civil War. He passed away several years ago, and the 'kids' are scattered all over the country, but I have one son that lives here on the farm.

"We had a hard time clearin' off the land and makin' our farm. It wuz government land here in the wild woods, that we homesteaded, and we had to make everything.

"I have never traveled anywhere, nor been anywhere in all my life. I have jist stayed at home, worked hard, and took care of the 'kids.' People these days don't know nothin' about raising families. Times are too modern, and they druther raise poodle dogs than babies.

"I never had a doctor in my house when my eleven 'kids' wuz born. Us ol' mothers in the neighborhood allers took care and waited on each other. Nowdays they all have to go to a hospital and lay under a doctor's care, and as soon as it is all over they get up, put on starchy clothes, trigger up and primp, and put the babies on a bottle and leave them in somebody else's care while they go some place.

"I allers got more satisfaction out of settin' around and smokin' my ol' pipe in the evening after my work wuz done, an' watchin' the 'kids' play, than to go out and lolly-gag around as they do nowdays."

L.L. Broadfoot

The Modern Maid

This is a portrait of Iris Street of Salem, Missouri, who smokes her cigarette in perfect contentment as she states:

"I don't understand why our old grandmothers are so hard against we girls who smoke cigarettes.

"They think it's terrible to see us with a cigarette in our fingers, and at the same time and while criticizing us, they sit before the fireplace with their legs crossed, a chew of long, green hillside tobacco in one jaw, and their long stem pipe sticking in the other, and there they envelop themselves in a screen of strong blue smoke, and chew and spit, as they discuss their horrors for the modern maid and her cigarette.

"I'd much rather smell the smoke from a mild cigarette, than that which passes through the stem of an old clay pipe that has been used for years and has become strong enough to walk."

John Counts

Reynolds County, Missouri

JOHN SAYS:

"I am three-quarters Indian, an' I'm seventy-four years ol', an' a 'bow an' arr fisherman' by profession. My home is jist anywhere in the Ozark hills, but I am a native of Reynolds County, Mo.

"I fish with 'bow an' arr' an' I make 'em myself. They are made ov cedar wood, an' the spikes are made ov ol' worn out files that I pick up here an' there, take 'em into the shop, an' hammer 'em out into a nice spearhead or spike.

"I am knowed all through the Missouri Ozarks an' parts ov Arkansaw as 'ol' fisherman John Counts.' I know all the streams in the Missouri Ozarks an' North Arkansaw like a book, an' have waded an' fished in about all ov 'em.

"I never use a boat. I wade around kinder slow an scare the fish out frum under rocks, logs, an' ol' tree roots, an' shoot 'em on the run; an', boy, I can git 'em! I can plunk a perch between the eyes fifty feet away!

"I hardly ever miss a shot, an' I've killed a heap ov squirrels an' turkeys with my ol' 'bow an' arr.' My paap wuz an expert with 'bow an' arr,' an' he larned me how to make 'em an' use 'em; an' he killed a heap ov deer; he killed big deer; an' I've killed big turkeys too, an' a whole lot ov squirrels.

"I sleep out lots ov nights along the rivers an' creeks in the Ozarks—I sleep under big sycamore trees on white gravel bars, an' watch fer squirrels; an' when I see one runnin' grapevines or jumpin' frum tree to tree, I pick up my 'bow an' arr,' an' I shoot 'im; an' I make a fire an' brile 'im on a stick. If I can, I get a sassafras stick 'cause sassafras gives the meat a better flavor.

"I kill big heaps ov fish an' squirrels an' give 'em to the peepuls along the streams where I go, 'cause they like me—they know 'ol' fisherman John,' an' they are my friends.

"I used to do lots ov fishin' in a little crooked mountain stream called 'Big Creek' in northeast Shannon Co., Mo., fer a man by the name ov Swiney—ol' Judge Jim Swiney ov Rat, Mo., who ran a little country store an' post office.

"Judge Swiney would have country picnics an' basket dinners, an' would hire me to come an' kill fish fer 'im.

"He had a son named Ben. He'd say, 'Now, John, I want you to fish fer me today, an' Ben, I want you to go along an' carry the fish fer John, an' actually, I have loaded that boy down with fish till he couldn't walk.

"I'm gettin' purty old, but I still love the sport, an' the Ozarks has been a wonderful home fer me."

50

51

Jeff Frizzell

JEFF SAYS:

"I am sixty-five years old. I wuz born in Richwood, Mo., an' pa an' ma moved to Knotwell, near Newburg, Mo., when I wuz ten years old. Later we moved to Sligo, where me an' pa got a job cuttin' cord wood, an' workin' in the coalin' pits at the ol' iron furnace. We only got twenty-five cents a cord for choppin' wood an' it took a real he-man to chop two cords a day.

"I never got no schoolin', 'cause I wuz forced to leave school when I wuz ten years old to help pa make a livin' fer the family. I wuz only in the second grade, an' had nothin' but the old blue-back speller to study an' now I have forgot everything I knowed, an' I hain't got no education a-tall.

"I run this little fillin' station an' the way I keep books is this: 'I lay out a nail fer each gallon of gas I sell durin' the day, an' in the evenin' all I got to do is count my nails an' know jist how many gallons I've sold. If I should have forty nails, that shows that I have sold forty gallons that day.'

"I attended school at Fishwater, Mo., an' wuz jist gettin' started good when pa moved away. We had to go where we could get some work to do and we thought Sligo would be a good place, 'cause the ol' iron works wuz goin' in full blast an' they needed men to chop cord wood an' work in the coalin' pits. But we wuzn't there long until Cleveland wuz elected president of the U. S., an' the works all shut down an' throwed us all out of work, an' it wuz the hardest times I ever se'ed.

"Me an' Mary live alone in this log cabin by the roadside an' make our livin' with this little fillin' station. We've been married a long time an' live happy. I am not a drinkin' man. I never drunk enough whisky to even feel it, an' I never drunk a bottle of beer in my life, but I got to have my coffee or I can't go. I don't guess I've got an enemy in this world, an' I've been here a long time."

Evening Shade School

Setting back upon a beautiful mountain slope, facing the east, amidst the deep dark shade of a dense cedar forest in the hills of southeast Phelps County, near Edgar Springs, Missouri, is a little log schoolhouse known as "Evening Shade School."

This tiny log structure, and the only schoolhouse of its kind known to the artist and writer, was built—according to the statement of an elderly lady who lives near by—about one hundred years ago, or prior to Civil War Days. It has only one door, and two windows, and a floor space of about sixteen by twenty feet, with a nine-foot log ceiling, and is very quaintly equipped, having only old-fashioned, long straight benches, with no desks or any place in which to place books and school supplies, and a seating capacity of about twenty pupils.

On the wall in front is the old-fashioned wooden blackboard upon which the pioneer educators gave instruction in reading, writing, and arithmetic. Upon the roof, over the door, still hangs the old bell, that almost a century ago rang out its sound, and echoed its call to the pioneer boys and girls of the hills, who, in tattered clothes and bare feet, carrying lunch baskets, slates, and blue-back spelling books, trekked over the winding mountain trails from all directions, leading up to the door to where they sat under the clapboard roof of this little ramshackle hut so cozily nestled under the low-swinging branches of the evergreen forest, to acquire what they termed, 'the old blue-back speller education.' By this they meant that the only book they had to study was the blue-back speller.

People in rural communities were taught in those days that the only essential in education for one's future well-being was to know how to read, write and figure, and that, that was all the education required upon which to build a successful future, and now, while in conversation with the pioneer fathers and mothers, they are frequently heard to say, "Well, I hain't got nothin' only jist a blue-back speller education, 'cause pa and ma said that if we learned to read and write, that wuz good enough."

This little pioneer house of education so gorgeously wrapped in nature's beauty of evergreen trees, and wild mountain roses, has served as an all-purpose building for community gatherings such as church, box suppers, Christmas trees, community sings, etc., and now since it is no longer used for school purposes, it is said it is used for funeral services, after which the deceased is laid to rest there in the large public cemetery, seen in the immediate background which is about three hundred yards from the schoolhouse.

Donald McGuirck

In the hills of Dent Co., Missouri

DONALD SAYS:

"I am only twelve years old but I would shore like to have a job so I could help pa make a livin' for our family. There's eleven of us—pa and ma, and nine of us kids—and we have it purty tough at our home.

"Pa works on the WPA job a little, once in a while, but they don't give him enough of it to do much good, and I've got a brother in the CCC camp, but we don't have near enough to eat on what they both make, and I wish I could get a job and help out.

"We live in this little house, built of logs and lumber, and it's too small for our family. It has only two rooms and that hain't enough for all of us kids, and when winter comes it's awful bad.

"Us kids go barefoot all summer long and don't get any shoes till late in the fall and sometimes nearly Christmas, when it's gettin' purty cold. I don't mind it so much in the summertime, only when I have to go out in the hills.

"Ma takes the whole bunch of us and we go way back on these high hills and in the deep hollers to pick huckleberries and blackberries, and that shore is hard on bare feet, 'cause we get briars in our legs and sometimes step on a snake.

"If we didn't gather berries, kill rabbits and squirrels, and do things like that, I guess we couldn't live at all.

"I would like to go to a big town once, and see how people live there, but I don't guess they live like we do.

"I see people from the city once in a while, and I think they act awful funny, and I wonder what they do for a livin'.

"I hain't never been nowhere in my life and I get awful blue and would like to leave the country, but when will I ever get a break."

56

L L Broadfoot

57

Preacher John F. Lewis

Rector, Missouri

PREACHER LEWIS SAYS:

"I am jist an ol' fashioned hill preacher—the kind that roams all through the Ozarks ov southern Missouri, an' preach the gospel truth to the people in the little schoolhouse that stands upon the hill.

"I believe in the ol' 'glory halle-lu-jah' kind ov religin, that makes 'em jump up an' down, an' shout an' holler an' scream like a panther.

"I never went to school any, but I carry my Bible with me jist the same. I've hearn lots of scripture quoted, an' I can remember well, an' can quote frum what I've hearn, an' can preach a sermon that makes the congregation bile over with that ol' hot religin that makes 'em scramble, hug, an' love each other.

"The trouble is, we've got too many ov these 'high-hat, high-priced preachers goin' around all shiny an' slicked up, wearin' a fried shirt with a white collar standin' so high their nose sticks through the buttonhole, that don't preach the Bible or tell the people the truth. All they care about is that cigar, whisky, and dance money they get for preachin', and they're not out to save souls.

"Boy, them kind ov preachers won't debate the question with ol' John F. Lewis! When I get hold ov 'em, I make the smoke fly, get 'em cornered, an' make 'em take a tree.

"It does me good to pop a few questions an' show 'em how little they know about the Bible. Sich durned preachers as that, I hain't got no use fer 'em! They ort to be at home carryin' slop to the pigs, or cleanin' out the barn, or somethin'.

"I don't preach fer money, I preach to heal sick souls, raise 'em up, an' put 'em on the right road home. Ov course, if a brother asks me to go home with 'em an' stay all night after church, I might do that, an' eat two or three or four meals with 'im, but I never pass the hat.

"When ye want to go to church where folks have a good time, jist come down among the ol' brothers an' sisters ov the Ozarks an' watch that ol' pot ov religin bile over when I deliver my sermon, then close by singin' that good ol' hymn, 'I'm goin' home to die no more.'"

59

Jess Thompson

The Man Who Kills Squirrels With Rocks

JESS SAYS:

"I'll bet I can kill more squirrels with rocks than most fellers can with a gun! Now, boys, I can really knock 'em. I am fifty-four years old and cain't throw as good as I used to, an' sometimes I have to throw three or four times before I get 'em, but I'll shore knock 'em; an' if they run in a hole so I can't knock 'em out with rocks, I jist climb the tree an' take a little stick an' twist 'em out an' take 'em by the tail an' rap 'em against the tree an' kill 'em.

"I clumb a tree one day, an' pulled four squirrels out ov one hole. Hit's plum easy for me to get all the squirrels I want, an' don't have to pay nary a cent fer ammunition.

"These little gray squirrels are plenty hard to hit sometimes when they're runnin' grapevines. I've killed lots of wild turkeys with rocks, too, an' 'possums an' coons, boy! I jist wish you could see all ov 'em in a pile that I have knocked out ov these trees with rocks.

"When I go fishin' I never use hooks an' gigs an' things. All I do is jist wade around very slow an' feel around under rocks, an' logs, an' ol' tree roots, an' catch all the fish I want with my hands. Pa an' ma used to have a time with me. I'd steal away frum 'em an' be gone all day long out in the hills an' when I would come back in the evenin' I'd be loaded down with fish or squirrels. I'd meet people an' they'd ask how I'd get the squirrels, an' I'd tell 'em an' they wouldn't believe me. Squirrels didn't get too high in these trees fer me to knock 'em out with rocks even when I wuz only fourteen or fifteen years ol'!

"I had to go barefooted until I wuz twenty-two an' boy! I've plowed these rocks all over the hills with my bare feet, an' knocked my toenails off, but it made no difference, I kept on goin'. Lots ov times I'd walk the hills all day an' throw rocks till I'd be tired an' then I'd lay down an' kiver myself up in leaves an' go to sleep, an' my ol' dog would lay by me.

"I would usually take some salt along in my pocket, an' when I got hungry, I'd make up a fire an' brile a squirrel. They are shore good when you brile 'em on sassafras or hickory sticks."

Mrs. Clementine Hance

Age 75

Phelps County, Missouri

"I was born in McMinn County, Tennessee, April 21, 1866. I came to Missouri when I was twelve years old, and have lived in the hills of Phelps County ever since.

"I raised eleven 'kids' and my husband passed away when the 'kids' were all small. I have lived on a farm all my life, an' besides doin' my own work an' takin' care of the 'kids' of my own, I have minded my sister's 'kids' while she spun, wove and knitted, and made clothes.

"Us ol' mothers had to help one another, an' if we hadn't, we never would'a got through, 'cause it shore was tough pickin's fer us compared to what people have today. But after all, I druther live back in the ol' ox-trail days. In them days we had to work hard and wear our ol' homespun linsey clothes, but today they don't wear none a-tall.

"I live three miles from Newburg, and I walk the whole round, an' do my tradin', and get back home in time to chop wood to do overnight.

"The ol' generation that settled in this country an' had to clean up their land and make their homes railly know what hardships mean, and the few of us that are left are still as tough as a whalebone an' can stand more than the young people of today who scamper about the streets at night, smoke cigarettes, and drink beer."

63

Jim Talley

Age 82—Bangert, Missouri

JIM SAYS:

"I wuz born an' raised in Overton County, Tennessee, where I lived a neighbor to Secretary of State Cordell Hull, when we wuz boys.

"I knowed all the Hull family well. They air the workin'est people I ever see'd. We lived close together and me an' Cordell's pappy used to raft lumber an' logs down the Obey River, and Cordell went along many times an' helped us. He wuz a boy that wuz allers hustlin' around doin' somethin'.

"I knowed 'im when he wuz elected to his first office, an' that wuz the office of prosecuting attorney of Overton County, where we lived.

"I allers noticed him and he never wuz beat fer nothin'. When he run fer office, he allers got it.

"His pappy wuz a fine man an' a hard worker, an' he had a mighty good mother, too. They wuz good neighbors.

"I left Tennessee an' come to Missouri fifty-five years ago, an' I have allers wished that I had took Cordell's pappy's advice and stayed in Tennessee.

"I wrote a letter to Cordell since he has been apinted to this high giverment office, an' he answered an' wrote me an awful good letter, an' said as how he would like to see me, an' about our ol' boyhood days together in Tennessee, an' ast me to come to Washington, D. C., an' see him.

"It made me feel awful good to know he still remembered me, an' wuzn't stuck up too high to notice me, but I have never been up an' see'd him yet.

"I see his picture in the papers once in a while, an' I notice there is some changes in 'im to what there wuz when I knowed 'im, an' some of these pictures jist don't look like 'im at all.

"Well, hit's funny at the difference in people. Now there we wuz, boys together, an' here I am settin' down here in the Ozarks, smokin' an ol' cob pipe, an' there he is, settin' at the head of our giverment, smokin' the finest cigars.

"This shore does seem funny, when we wuz jist little ol' ragged boys together, but that's the way this ol' world goes. We cain't all be big men an' do big things, but hit kinder gits my goat to think about it."

Eugene Curtis

Jadwin, Missouri

Mr. Curtis Says:

"Well, I am beginnin' to git up in years. I am seventy-eight years ol', an' my wife thirty-eight. We have eight children—a baby three months ol', an' the oldest one fourteen years.

"It keeps me nippin' an' tuckin' to make a livin' fer 'em at my age. We jist have a little rough patch ov land, a few chickens an' a cow, but our chief support is the ol' age pension, an' since I'm gettin' too ol' to work, I have got to take care ov myself an' live as long as possible fer the pension; fer what would my family do if I should die?

"I am a craftsman an' have sold lots ov my work that brought in money fer the family, but my hands are crippled up with rheumatism now till I can no longer do that.

"Here are some samples of my work. This is what I call my 'blind man's walkin' cane,' an' a chain. The walkin' cane is made ov walnut timber, an' the chain is cedar.

"Look 'em over! There's real art in this work, an' I done it all with my ol' pocketknife.

"I got a letter from a man in Colorado Springs, Colorado, a few days ago who wanted me to make up a shipment ov walkin' canes like this, an' send them to him, an' he would pay me a good price fer 'em, but my hands are crippled up too much.

"People often ask me how we git along an' make a livin' fer such a big family, but we do it somehow, an' I see other families with only two or three kids that don't seem to git along any better than we do, an' if we had two dozen, there would be some way of gittin' along.

"I think God intended fer us to raise big families. I don't believe in birth control, an' if we don't wake up to our duty, an' git in, in the ol' fashioned way, an' raise big families as we used to, the niggers, the Jews, an' Dagoes are going to dominate America, an' we'll take the back seat.

"No doubt, I'll die a poor man, but when I enter the pearly gates of heaven I can face Saint Peter with a clear conscience that I have done my part in populatin' the earth."

66

L.L. Broadfoot

Pete Counts

"The Hill Comedian"

Reynolds County, Missouri

PETE SAYS:

"Well, I'm jist a common ol' hill billy singer an' fiddler, an' here I am, singin' the 'Squallin' Cat.' You see, I make up all the songs I play an' sing, sich as, 'Liza Jane,' 'Black-eyed Susie,' 'Squallin' Cat,' 'Comin' Through the Rye,' 'Hell Among the Yearlings,' 'Hell Up Skunk River,' an' all ov them there ol' tunes ye hear around in these hills.

"Here in this ol' box house, is where I made this ol' fiddle, an' the first one I ever owned. I call it my 'horse hair fiddle,' an' hit hain't nothin' but jist a flat board with hair that I pulled frum the ol' mare's tail an' stretched over it fer strings, an' I made the bow the same way.

"Hit wuz on this ol' board fiddle that I larned to play all these ol' tunes. People come frum all around through the hills to hear me fiddle an' sing, an' cut up an' act a fool. They call me the 'Hill Comedian.'

"I hain't got nairy bit ov educashun nor I hain't nairy bit purty, but I feel good, an' can make people laff. They say that 'beauty is only skin deep,' so maybe I'd be purty if you'd skin me—anyway, I enjoy life an' have a good time. When they have picnics an' gatherin's ov any kind around in the Ozarks, they allers have ol' Pete there if they can git me to come.

"I can whistle an' imitate birds ov all kinds. I can hoot like an owl, caw like a crow, whistle like a mockin' bird, an' all them things, an' lots ov times I'm out listenin' at the birds sing, an' I start whistlin' like 'em, an' soon I've got a tune started before I know it.

"A feller can larn a lot ov things in a purty simple way as he goes through life if he'll jist try; an' you don't haf to be all purty an' polished up neither, to be attractive.

"I am as happy as a lark, but I guess I look worse than the 'Devil peepin' through a brush pile.' My womern says, 'I'm the purtiest little thing she ever see'd when the light's blowed out.' Hit wuz my dove eyes, an' pigeonhole mouth, an' birdlike voice that caused her to larn to love an' marry me. I never had to ask her to marry me but once, till she grabbed me an' said, 'Oh shore, sweet Pete! an' I know we can make a good livin' too, 'cause you are a good singer, fiddler, an' whistler, an' I can take in washin's, while you go around singin', fiddlin', an' whistlin' fer soap, an' we'll be two ov the happiest an' most prosperous little humpy-dumpies in these hills.' An' I grabbed her, hugged an' kissed her, an' said, 'O.K. sweet lollipop, that's a trade, an' I'll get you a good washboard an' tub too, an' we'll go fifty-fifty an' get married an' live happy.' So we did, an' we've done purty well, only a few times when she'd have to wait on me a little while fer the soap, 'cause once in a while I might feel bad or get a little blue or somethin' an' cain't whistle very good, an' that holds up the washin'."

68

L L Broadfoot

69

Alva Leech

Lake Springs, Missouri

Mr. Leech Says:

"I will soon be ninety-three years old. I wuz born in Lawrence County, Illinois, November 19, 1848, an' come to Missouri in 1870, just shortly after I wuz married, an' six years after the Civil War had ended. Times wuz purty tollerable hard and money wuz as scarce as hen's teeth.

"We had one horse, one mule, an' a yoke of oxen. We worked 'em all together an' come to Missouri in a covered wagon, an' wuz seventeen days comin' through.

"It wuz purty aggravatin' to work oxen, mules, an' horses together, but that wuz the only way we had of gettin' here.

"We crossed the Mississippi River on a ferryboat at St. Louis, where Eads Bridge now stands. They were just settin' the piers and beginnin' to build the bridge at that time.

"When the Civil War broke out in 1861, I had three brothers that had to go. How terrible this wuz, an' my brothers wuz killed too! My father wuz a cooper by trade an' didn't have to go to war, but was put into a barrel factory to work. His services there wuz considered worth more to the government.

"I wuz only thirteen years old an' wuz left on the farm to make a livin' for the family. It wuz up-hill business for a boy my age to work oxen an' do the farm work as we had to do in them days, but I had to do it just the same.

"I fell in love with a neighbor girl and wuz married in 1870, and started to Missouri. When we landed here, we hardly knowed what to do—nothin' but wild woods and wild animals.

"I homesteaded a small tract of government land in Phelps County, an' we camped out an' slept out in our wagon under the stars for many days while I built a log hut. The wolves howled around our wagon, and we could hear the ol' wild mountain bobcat scrawl out in the hollers below us.

"The owls would sit on the branches of trees over our wagon and hoot all night long. We cooked our meals on campfires made of oak wood and pine knots. We would lie in our wagon at night and see the beautiful moon rise through the timber over the Ozark mountain tops, an' see the stars shoot across the blue heavenly skies. It wuz great days an' days that I love to think and talk about, and to you peepul who have never had experience in Ozark hill life, you don't know what you've missed.

"I only wish I could live ninety-three years more. Give me the Ozarks first, last, and always. It's God's wonder spot!"

Susie Pace

Crawford County, Missouri

MRS. PACE SAYS:

"I am seventy-nine years old. I was born on the Huzzah Creek in Crawford County, Missouri, August 3, 1862. My mammy commenced on me when I wuz jist a little towhead learnin' me how to work an' do things.

"You see, I didn't get no education, 'cause I never got to go to school. That wuz back in the Civil War days when peepul had somethin' else to do an' think about, besides goin' to school.

"Times wuz hard an' all we knowed wuz work, work, work. Mammy showed me how to piece quilts, an' I have done more of that in my life than anything else. It's the kind of work I love above all other, an' I have made hundreds an' hundreds of purty quilts.

"I save up all kinds of ol' worn-out clothes, an' by cuttin' them up into blocks an' sewin' them together, I have somethin' that's rail purty, 'cause there's all kinds of colors together, an' they make purty quilts. Handmade quilts are purtiest an' lots better than any other kind, an' it's a good way of workin' up your rags into somethin' useful.

"I have made a practice of savin' up empty spools, an' now I have seven hundred an' ninety-five spools hangin' on the wall, from which I have used the thread in the past fifteen years, an' I have done all this work by hand, too, an' didn't use no machine.

"Peepul laff at me 'cause I live an' dress in the ol'-fashion way, but I don't care. I guess I am ol'-fashioned. I don't go to movin' picture shows, nor I won't ride in an automobile either. I'd ruther walk, 'cause I am afeard of cars.

"I wear my dresses big an' loose, an' long enough to come clear down to my ankles, an' that looks funny to the young folks, an' when they want to dress clownish fer some kind of a funny party, they come an' borrow my clothes.

"They can laff at my long dresses if they want to, an' I don't care nairy bit, 'cause I'm not modern nor stuck up.

"I sometimes have a good laff at their modern short dresses too, an' specially when they go to bend over or sit down."

73

Ma's Quilting Bee

This is Mrs. Lizzie Fiebelman—"Ma" as everyone knows her—her three daughters, and two hired girls, engaged in making quilts by hand, at the Ozark Hotel in Salem, Mo.

Ma, who with her three daughters owns and operates the hotel, states:

"I was born and raised on a farm in Crawford County, Mo., and that's where I was taught, and learned to work, and where I raised my girls and taught them to work.

"We used to run a store at Dillard, Mo., and sold goods for many years, but we also lived on a farm at the same time. It kept us busy keeping up both ends, because we had a big bunch of stock on the farm to take care of; and we also had a big business at the store, as it was during the days when Sligo Iron Works were in full blast and lots of men working, and we got their checks, and made money.

"We have no boys in our family, so it was up to me and my husband and four daughters to run the farm and store, because we couldn't always hire the kind of help we needed. Sometimes we kept two hundred head of cattle on the farm, and my girls rode the Ozark range, looking after these cattle, salting them, and keeping them together; so, work is no scarecrow to us, for we know how to do it! My husband passed away a few years ago, and we sold the store and farm and all came to Salem and bought this hotel, and all work to run it. We make all of our quilts, sheets, and pillow cases, that we use in our hotel. We do our own laundry, and all of our own cookin'; and when you come to our hotel it's not like goin' and settin' down at a hot-dog counter, and goin' away growlin' 'cause you didn't get enough to eat, for we give you somethin' more than just a soup bone to gnaw, a glass of cold water, and a toothpick.

"Here, it's home cookin', homemade blankets, and home service, and you'll feel at home. We gather up and save all of our waste cloth, cut it into blocks, and piece it into quilt tops. We have all colors and all sorts of designs, and they are really beautiful."

Seated around the quilt, beginning at front to left, going around, are: Ma Fiebelman, Grace Fiebelman, Bessie McGuire, Bertha Fiebelman, Effie Fiebelman, and Mary Bell.

Josie Labrash

Dent County, Missouri

Josie, who is an expert in handling the old wool cards, says:

"I have done everything in the handlin' ov wool frum shearin' it frum the ol' sheep's back, to knittin' it into gloves, stockin's, an' clothes. Pappy used to make me go out an' shear sheep all day long, an' I'd come in, in the evenin', all tired out, an' jist stinking like a dad-burned ol' sheep; then mammy would make me set up till nigh onto midnight an' pick the cockleburs out ov the wool, wash it, an' get the dad-burn stuff ready fer the cards the next day.

"If you know, or have ever had anything to do with cockleburs an' know how tight they'll stick to your pants, then picture yourself tryin' to pick 'em out ov wool! Why gosh-durn! I would druther wake up on a rainy Monday mornin' with a bad case ov 'cramp-colic,' or with wash day on my mind than to have sich a job.

"If there wuz a law passed givin' people sentences ov so many weeks or months pickin' cockleburs out ov wool instead ov hangin' 'em or sendin' 'em to the pen fer life, there wouldn't be so much meanness done.

"My mammy used to make me card the wool while she spun it into yarn threads, when I wuzn't bigger than a guinea pig. We allers had to knit all the gloves an' socks fer pappy an' all the boys at home.

"I have allers handled cotton the same as I have wool, an' where we had to take cockle-burs out of wool, we had to take the seed out ov cotton, but hit warn't near so bad a job 'cause pa made some ol' hand jins that we used in takin' the seeds out ov cotton, but I've even cranked them dad-burn things till I'd get dizzy an' could see stars, an' wish they warn't no sich thing as cotton.

"We raised the cotton ourselves, so I've follered it from the field to the loom, then made it into shirts, pants, skirts, drawers, an' sich like.

"Lord God! People don't know nothin' these days. If all ov our fathers and mothers could rise up an' see how different things air an' what this silly generation is doin', they'd faint an' fall back in their graves.

"I still use my ol' cards, an' can handle 'em in more ways than a monkey can handle a peanut! But I've handled 'em all my life, since a little tot, an' ov course, a feller ort to learn a little in that time."

76

Mrs. Vina Boxx

Wife of Henry

Elsinore, Butler County, Missouri

Mrs. Boxx Says:

"Henry splits clapboards an' kivers houses, an' I keep the ol' spinnin' wheel hummin' to help make a livin', an' it seems like it keeps us both busy to keep the wolf frum the door, an' keep goin'; but I've allers hear'n that 'where there's a will, there's a way,' an' I guess that's right, 'cause we hain't never starved to death yet.

"I go about through the neighborhood an' other places, gatherin' up all the gunny sacks I can find. I bring 'em home, sit down and ravel 'em out, an' take the threads an' twist 'em together on my ol' spinnin' wheel, an' knit 'em into rugs, scarfs, an' other things, an' sell an' trade 'em for food an' clothes.

"They make fine floor rugs, dresses, scarfs, an' things. I color 'em up in different colors an' they are rail purty too. So you see how, by hustlin', you can go around an' pick up things other people throw away, an' make something purty an' useful out ov it.

"I believe in helpin' our husbands, an' doin' things to make homes what they ort to be.

"So many wimern these days that don't try to help their man do nothin', an' are jist as useless as a knot on a stump, an' all they care about is to polliwog around here an' there, an' ever time they hear a car 'honk,' stick their head out the winder to see if it's somebody after 'em to go some place.

"Sich 'pleg-goned wimern' as that, hain't no good fer wives, an' that's why the courts are filled with divorce cases. I never see'd the like in my life!

"I can take my ol' spinnin' wheel an' go out on top ov one ov these high Ozark peaks an' live out on a flat rock under a shade tree an' make a livin'; an' anybody else can too that's got the quality ov hustlin', an' wants to do the right thing instead ov skinnin' through winders an' dodgin' out back doors at night to hoo-doo their husband while he's killin' himself at work.

"T'other day I went out an' in jist a little while, I had gathered up enough gunny sacks to make two or three dollars woth ov scarfs an' rugs, an' right now I'm workin' 'em up.

"Me an' Henry have allers been hard workin' critters, an' while we hain't got no finery, yet, we hain't starvin' neither, an' we'll get by somehow with our spinnin' wheel, frow, an' mallet."

L C Broadfoot

Mrs. Delilah McKeethlen

Dillard, Missouri

MRS. McKEETHLEN SAYS:

"I am eighty years ol' an' have knit stockin's, gloves, an' sweaters, an' have woven linsey clothes an' carpets on the ol' hand loom ever since I wuz knee high to a duck.

"Ma used to make me sit up till nigh on to midnight an' knit socks when I wuz only fifteen years ol', an' I got to where I could knit a sock or glove as quick as she could.

"I still enjoy the ol' way of workin' an' doin' things. Of course, there's a heap of difference in the way things are done today, to what they were when I wuz a girl, but sometimes I get disgusted with this stuff they call 'modern life,' an' feel that I would like to see peepul come down a notch an' live in the ol' style again.

"I do my own cannin' an' put up all my own fruits an' vegetables for winter. I go out to the cornfield an' pick my apron full of beans, an' come in an' set up late at night an' hull beans by hand.

"I help to do the butcherin' an' cure the bacon. I dry apples an' pumpkin an' sack them up for winter's use.

"I go back in the hills an' pick huckleberries an' blackberries, an' can them up to make pies for Christmas, an' along at that time of the year we have a regular ol' 'home-comin',' an' all my 'kids,' my grandchildren an' great grandchildren gather in, an' we have the rail true Christmas spirit.

"We have church an' Christmas tree in the little country schoolhouse, an' there Santa Claus hands out presents to all the 'kids.'

"I think us country peepul live a happier life than city peepul do. Down here in the hills we live as neighbors an' do for each other, an' in the city they seem to live to do each other.

"I sometimes think it's awful the way things are goin' an' wonder what this ol' world is comin' to.

"I'd ruther live outdoors an' sleep under a shade tree with nothin' to eat but corn bread an' sorghum molasses if I can live in peace an' go to church, than to have all the wealth on earth, an' live in a mad ol' world where you hear nothin' but war, war, war."

L L Broadfoot

81

Bob Derryberry

Akers, Missouri

"I am eighty-two years old and have spent my life in the jungles ov the Ozarks, workin', makin' baskets, diggin' roots, an' doin' a little of this and a little of that, to get by on and raise my family.

"You see this basket? Well, I've been makin' 'em ever since I was a little towhead. My wife makes 'em, too, but she makes a different kind.   I make these out ov white oak timber, and they are railly good, too, an' last furever.

"The farmers use them to feed out ov. They carry corn in 'em, an' the women use them to pick up chips in, and carry in taters, an' cabbage, an' beans frum the garden, an' they air good fer a lot of things around the house.

"I sell the bushel baskets fer one dollar, an' the half bushel basket fer fifty cents. Course that hain't no money, but it helps out, an' all them things count when ye air just livin' by the skin ov yer teeth anyway.

"I raise a little terbacker patch every year an' sell a few twists ov terbacker, an' that helps ter keep the ol' wolf frum the door.

"I have wondered a lot ov times jist how I got by an' raised my family, but if a feller is handy about doin' things, the Ozarks is a purty good place ter live, 'cause ye can find material ter make most anything ye want."

E. L. Broadfoot

Malinda Derryberry

Wife of Bob Derryberry

Akers, Missouri

MRS. DERRYBERRY SAYS:

"Bob has told you about the baskets he makes an' how handy they are for the farmers to use about their premises, an' now I'm goin' to tell you about the ones I make an' what they're good for.

"My baskets are made of roots from buckbrush—'Beaver brush' some people call 'em, an' I do this by takin' the roots, boilin' 'em in water, peelin' all the rough outerbark off, leavin' 'em perfectly white, then I dip 'em in different colors of dye, an' brade 'em into baskets by hand.

"The buckbrush root is a very substantial material for makin' baskets, an' makes a beautiful piece of work.

"They have that real lastin' quality, an' you will see my baskets on sale here an' there through the Ozarks.

"While Bob's baskets are used by the farmers, mine are used by the farmers' wives for egg baskets, sewing baskets, an' to sit on tables to put all kinds of trinkets in.

"I make several different sizes, an' ornament 'em in different colors an' different ways to beautify 'em.

"People from the cities drive down through the Ozarks an' peep down upon our little log cabins in the hollers below, as they drive around the high divides in their fine automobiles, an' wonder how we make a livin' down here in the wilds, but you cain't get ahead of the old hill billy, for the most of us have some scheme, trick, or trade that gits us by.

"We know a little somethin', whether we look like it or not, an' we've allers got the material in the hills to make most anythin' we want or need."

Dillard Water Mill

Dillard, Missouri

This old-fashioned gristmill is owned and operated by Mr. L. E. Clemme, of Dillard, Mo.

Mr. Clemme states that it has been in operation longer than the government has any record of, and is still in good condition, and doing its daily turnout of the old-fashioned French burr corn meal.

It is located in a very picturesque spot deep in the hills of Crawford County, on the Big Huzzah Creek, and gets its power from the rapid rushing waters of this stream as it winds its way down through the Crawford County mountains, spouting into the giant over-shot water wheel.

It abounds in nature's beauty, in the deep, narrow, winding valley of the Big Huzzah, between chains of rugged, lofty hills running north and south, and densely wrapped in foliage of various kinds and colors with the dark evergreen of tall pine and cedar piercing the blue skies in the far distance.

It would seem that nature has provided this rugged natural setting exclusively for the old water mill—the high waterfalls and cliff rocks, a cove in the mountain side with back walls of solid stone, a natural foundation with high cornerstone laid by the hand of nature, upon which the mill is built, and a deep fissure or channel in the rock, which carries the water around to where it spouts forcefully into the wheel—and all this as completely arranged as if planned by skilled engineers.

A high stone wall across the stream—one of nature's own construction—provides a dam, making a beautiful reservoir of head waters from which the mill gets its power.

From over this dam, the Big Huzzah tosses its waters, foaming and sparkling, and rapidly rushing away to a distance of about two hundred feet and near by the mill to where it again forms into a natural bowl of deep blue, crystal clear water.

This giant bowl is about 150 feet wide, by three hundred feet in length, very deep, blue, and beautiful in form, and surrounded by a wide border of white gravel which seems to bid for the attention of campers and picknickers, and is a splendid place to fish.

Ozarkians frequently gather here to swim, to have Sunday school picnics and basket dinners, and to boil eggs on Easter day. Young folks often gather here to have marshmallow and wiener roasts at night.

There can be seen about the premises, old discarded hand-chiseled millstones that were imported here from France, and other relics that were used years and years ago, in the manufacturing of corn meal.

Standing all around are beautiful trees of various kinds with branches bowed, touching the roof of the old mill shed—the white oak, black oak, the maple, walnut, and sycamore; and is well known as one of nature's great beauty spots.

Goin' to Mill

This is Mr. A. O. Weaver as he was seen on his mule, with a sack of corn strapped to his saddle, a gun in his hand, and his hound-dogs following along, as he winds his way around the bluff up Current River Valley, on his way to the old Cedar Grove gristmill, to have his corn ground into meal.

Mr. Weaver says:

"We've got to have corn meal at our house or we can't live. I've got a big family an' it takes lots ov bread, an' when I go to mill, I allers take my gun an' dogs along an' by the time I make the round an' get back home, I've usually got a bunch of squirrels tied to this ol' white mule, an' that shore helps a lot at our table 'cause we all like wild meat, sich as fish, squirrels, 'possums an' 'coons an' ground hogs, an' turkeys.

"There's a plenty ov all kinds ov small game around up these river bottoms except turkey, an' we hain't got many ov them any more, so I don't know what my family would do if we lived where we couldn't have things like that to eat.

"The Ozarks is a grand ol' place to live, an' ov course we wuz all raised here, an' don't know nothin' else.

"This ol' Cedar Grove mill is a real ol' timer an' has been grindin' out corn meal ever since long before the Civil War. It has purtnye raised my family 'cause there is where I've allers took my corn to have it made into meal, an' it's the kind we all like, 'cause it's ground on the ol' French burrs.

"When I go to mill I allers tie my mule up an' while I'm waitin' fer my meal, I take my gun an' dogs an' go up on the hill an' shoot a few squirrels, or else I go down an' sit on the river bank an' fish a while.

"If it wasn't for fishin' tackles, guns, an' dogs, I don't know what us fellers way back in the hills would do, 'cause that's the way half ov us make our livin'!"

Making Sorghum

This is Ben Land and family in West Dent Co., Mo., making sorghum molasses.

Ben says:

"All the family have to work when molasses makin' time comes, but you can't hardly raise 'kids' on the farm without plenty of molasses and corn bread.

"We raise a big patch of cane every year and when the time comes to make the molasses in the fall, we all have to dig in and work until it's all finished. Some of us strip the blades from the cane, while others cut it and haul it to the mill, where one person feeds it into the mill which grinds out the juice. Another carries the juice and pours it into a pan for me to boil down and make into molasses.

"Our neighbors often get in and help, and we have a lot of fun at this time of year. Each time we stir off a batch of molasses, the 'kids' gather round and sop the pan.

"We have 'taffy pullin's' sometimes. The 'kids' all gather in and take molasses and cook it down to a stiff candy called 'taffy.' Two 'kids' will get out on the floor with one piece of taffy, and each will take an end of the piece in their teeth an' pull an' stretch an' eat it until it is all gone. The idea is to see who can eat the fastest and get the most candy. It's the durndest lot of fun you ever see'd."

W. S. Bland

Midridge, Missouri

Mr. Bland Says:

"Since our hogs are raised in the woods an' go wild here in the Ozarks, we have to drive 'em home once in a while an' mark their ears to tell whose hog it is.

"We do this as a means of identifyin' 'em. We take our pocket knife an' cut notches in their ears.

"Each feller has a different notch to the other feller. There has been many a dispute, a fight, an' even law suits over hogs, here in the hills, 'cause they were not marked an' everybody claimed 'em.

"These hogs git purty wild, an' have that ol' 'fightin' blood' in 'em, an' sometimes when we drive 'em in home, the 'kids' have to climb the fence, an' the dogs run under the house.

"It takes about all the family to mark a pig—one boy to hold its legs, while another cuts its ears, an' still another to take a club an' mind the ol' sow off, an' two more to catch another pig to have ready fer the knife.

"You'd be surprised how vicious an' tough these ol' Razor-backed ridge trotters git. Their tusks grow long an' crooked an' stick out at the sides of their mouth, which makes a real weapon.

"You ort to see one of 'em fight. They put all four feet together, an' throw their back up in a roll that looks like a circle saw, an' whirl round an' round with their mouth open, an' if they git a cut at a dog or wolf, they really leave 'em in bad shape.

"Some of 'em can stand on a quarter an' whip a dog or wolf purty easy.

"We call 'em 'ridge trotters' cause you usually see 'em high up on the ridges or main divides trottin' along all alone, an' about every two hundred yards, they stop, throw their heads high, an' stand for a minute, apparently listenin' fer somethin'.

"They seem to be a kind of picket or guard fer the rest of the herd. They can hear an acorn fall a quarter of a mile away an' can git there an' git it before it stops rollin'.

"But these are purty good hogs, an' make purty good meat, only a little tough sometimes."

Range Hogs in the Ozarks

Far back in the Current River hills near Timber, Mo., lies a long, deep winding hollow well known to the natives as "Hog Cave Holler," which branches off from another lengthy, rugged canyon known as "Happy Holler," leading up from Sinkin Creek in northeast Shannon County.

The Hog Cave Holler takes it's name from a cavern under a cliff rock high upon the mountain side where the wild range hogs take refuge against the cold winter winds, and sleep at night.

This natural housing place provides first-class sleeping quarters for many hogs at a time, and shelters them from cold rains and drifting snow storms.

It is well known as a place where hill dwellers go to get a trace of their hogs that have been gone for so long, and by crawling easily on their hands and knees for hundreds of feet to where they can peep over the ledge rock, they are able to glance at the different brands and ear marks, and identify their own if it happens to be in the herd. Many times the alert wild hog looks up to see the hunter peering over the ledge, when suddenly he gives a snort that stampedes the entire herd, and they go leaping wildly down the brushy mountainside, ahead of Winchester fire by the hunter who is attempting to kill what he thinks is his hog.

Great numbers of these wild mountain rangers are farrowed in deep caverns back in the mountainsides, and are raised in the wild woods, and bear no marks or brands by which to be identified; and in this case, they may belong to whoever may happen to be the best hog hunter.

The natives usually choose the winter season as the best time of the year to hog hunt, and especially during times of heavy snowfall, as this provides a splendid chance for the hunter to trail the animals from different points to caverns where they take refuge against storms, and sleep at night.

In the summertime, the hog hunter prowls through the hills looking for the animal around cold mountain streams, and small mud puddles in the deep hollows. As this is the time of year when the days are hot and the old razor-back mother likes to take her family and go for a good cool mud bath or wallow in the water. Sometimes the hunter takes his dogs along when going out in search of the wild rangers, and when he discovers a bunch of hogs in the distance, he sneaks up as close as possible, puts the dogs after them, and the hogs huddle together, and with mouths wide open, their eyes glary and sparkling, and with hair standing straight up, they go round and round in a small circle, standing their ground, ready for a fight. In this way the hunter is able to get close up, and see whose hog it is.

He calls it "rallying the hogs." He'll say, "I rallied 'em." Many times the hogs are butchered in the woods and hauled home in wagons.

This drawing was made late one evening as the hogs were seen by the artist as they trekked in from their day's journey through the hills gathering acorns on which they live.

94

L. L. Broadfoot

George Atchison

Butchering Hogs

Hartshorn, Missouri

GEORGE SAYS:

"I allers hate to see butcher day come, 'cause it's the nastiest dad-blamed day I ever see'd, an' everybody has to work—even the cats an' dogs keep busy—but we cain't never tell when butcher day is comin' down here in the Ozarks, 'cause our hogs run wild in the woods, an' so we jist have to kill 'em when we can catch 'em.

"Now, I hain't see'd these hogs fere months an' months, till I happened to get a glance at 'em early this mornin' as they went around the hillside above the house, with their tails curled over their backs, at a high rate of speed, as if they wuz chasin' wolves or somethin'; so I grabbed my gun, an' called out all the 'kids' an' dogs an' took a short cut an' headed 'em off up on the main divide north of the house an' there's where the battle started an' we killed 'em an' hauled 'em in.

"Some of 'em are about four years old an' I don't know whether we can eat 'em or not. You take some of these ol' long-nose, screw-tail hazel splitters an' let 'em run these ridges fer a while, an' they git so dad-blamed tough you cain't stick a fork in their gravy—no matter how long you cook 'em.

"But after all, they are purty cheap meat, fer they don't cost us nothin'; they jist grow up in the woods like wild cats an' what we get is all clear profit.

"I can take a couple ov these ol long-nose, screw-tail ridge trotters an' put 'em out, an' soon have the woods full ov hogs; an' I can look at an ol' sow an' tell whether she would be a good woods boss or not.

"I usually judge 'em by the length ov their nose; an' if they are longer from their eyes to the end ov their nose than anywhere else, then you may know that they are well able to go into the woods an' defend themselves an' raise their flock, for they are real warriors an' can put up a fight.

"We butcher some 'em sometimes that are so dad-blasted tough we can hardly scrape the hair off after we've had 'em in a barrel ov 'bilin' hot water.'

"My dogs are plum afeard ov 'em till they are cut up an' ready to eat, an' then they're not too anxious to tie into 'em."

Mary Boxx

Doniphan, Missouri

"I am eighty-six years ol', but I have good health an' shore do feel good. I have allers made it a practice to get up early in the mornin', light my pipe, get out and take a good ol' fresh breath ov Ozark Mountain air, as I go about doin' my mornin' chores. An' I think I have purty good lungs, too, cause I call my pigs in frum the hills every mornin' an' shell corn to 'em, an' you know they can hear my voice a mile away, an' how they do come runnin' in.

"By doin' this my pigs allers knows where home is an' I never have ter get out an' hunt 'em. All I got to do is jist git out an' yell a few times, an' they know my voice an' waste no time in gittin' here.

"Sometimes we have lean years an' they ain't enough acorns in the woods fer 'em to live on, an' they jist have to have a little corn."

Dr. John Robert Huffer

Corn and Wart Doctor of the Ozarks

Turtle, Missouri

DR. HUFFER SAYS:

"You hear lots said about the Ozarks an' Ozarkians, but I reckon I know more people in these hills, an' have been in more Ozark counties an' homes than any other man ov my age, 'cause I have a profession that calls me out here an' there at all hours.

"I am seventy-three years ol', an' am known as the 'corn an' wart doctor' ov the Ozarks, an' can cure any case ov headache too by rubbin' my hands together till I git up the electricity, an' my hands become hot, then apply them gently to the patient's head, an' with a few light strokes ov rubbin', the pain leaves, an' the patient goes off to sleep. It is the electricity I have in me that does the work. I am full ov it.

"I cure all my own headaches the same way, an' for years an' years I have been goin' frum house to house, through the hills takin' off warts an' corns, bringin' relief to the sufferin'.

"I hain't made no money out ov it, but sometimes I git a chicken, a few eggs, a gallon ov molasses, or a little terbacker, but, after all, it's a lot ov pleasure to me to know that I am able to step into the ol' cabin homes an' remove frowns frum faces an' make glad hearts by liftin' that painful corn frum the ol toe, an' that's worth somethin'.

"Ol' sore achin' corns have caused many a fuss between husband an' wife 'cause a man may come in frum his work sometimes, an' say somethin' to his wife that don't sound jist right to her 'cause that ol' corn is givin' her fits, an' they git into a big fuss an' separate, when nothin' in the world caused it but the miserable ol' corn. So I think I have kept peace in many families jist that way.

"If you have a wart on the end ov your nose or some place, I can jist rub my finger over it gently, with a few hocus-pocus remarks, an' the wart magically disappears.

"The Ozarkians know me well an' are glad to see Dr. Huffer comin' when that ol' wart or corn is givin' 'em thunder."

Dr. John Robert Huffer, Corns And Warts Removed

Margaret Swiney

The Ozark Midwife

Sinkin, Missouri

"Mag," as everyone knows her, is seventy-three years old, weighs ninety-two pounds, and is extremely energetic. Mag says:

"Aside from all my housework, an' the work I have done out on the farm sich as plowin' an' plantin' the crops, cuttin' brush an' buildin' fence, pitchin' hay, makin' molasses, an' nailin' roofs on buildings, cuttin' an' haulin' cord wood, makin' rails, an' drivin' posts an' about everythin' else, I have, as midwife, waited on more than four hundred maternity cases an' delivered that many babies to this world, by ridin' my ol' mare an' side saddle through these hills at all hours in the night.

"I owned one mare I called 'Gray Doll.' She wuz a kind an' faithful ol' animal, an' served me for about eighteen years. The nights never got too dark nor too cold fer me an' ol' Gray Doll to go out every time anybody knocked on my door fer service.

"My friends an' neighbors have come from far an' near, throughout the hills, an' called on me at all hours an' all kinds of weather.

"Many times it would be two o'clock in the morning when someone would rap on my cabin door an' call fer me to go.

"The weather would be cold and blustry, but they needed me. Immediately I would jump out of bed, light the kerosene lamp, jirk my clothes on, an' run out to the barn to find ol' Gray Doll ready an' waitin' fer me.

"Sometimes I would have ten miles to go with nothin' but a trail to follow through the hills, an' so dark you could hardly see your hand before you, an' many times would be rainin' an' freezin', an' my shoes would freeze fast to the saddle stirrups before I would get there.

"These were all poor people. Sometimes I got a little pay, but most of the time no pay at all. But, they needed me so bad, an' I couldn't say 'no.' They wuzn't able to pay, but somebody had to help them. Many times I found them livin' in small log cabins with no floor, just the bare earth to live on, with spaces between the logs in the wall, wide enough to sling a cat through, an' the 'kids' all barefoot an' sleepin' on the beds made of oak leaves.

"I have seen some very pitiful sights through my experience, an' have studied over my life an' wondered how I have stood all this work an' exposure, an' I guess if I hadn't been as tough as 'Caesar's heel,' I wouldn't be livin' today. But, I still take care of sich cases an have the birth certificates to prove it. But I don't feel like gettin' out in the rain an' snow at all hours in the night as I once did, though I wish to be kind, and serve humanity."

102

L L Broadfoot

Mat Hogan and Family

Dent County, Missouri

MAT SAYS:

"They can all fly high and ride in their fast cars that want to, but I druther risk little Jack an' Pete to pull me an' my family through these hills. Hit's not a fast way, but hit's a shore way of gittin' there.

"We live a long way from town, but we git up early in the mornin' an' I feed this little mule an' jinny, an' throw the harness on 'em while my womern cooks breakfast, then we eat an' load the kids, and cream cans, an' eggs, an' strike out to town. Hit's a slow way of travelin', but we don't have to stop an' clean spark plugs an' fix other things.

"Most of these fellers that whizz by in their autermobiles like a streak of 'greased lightnin' 'hain't got their ol' cars paid fer, an' yet they feel stuck up, an' laff at me 'cause I drive my little team of jackasses. But, by-Ned, there hain't no mortgage hangin' over these little donkies, an' we allers manage to git there, too.

"If everybody had to slow down a little, I think the whole world would be better off by a durned sight. The trouble is, we still have plenty of jackasses workin' in the harness, but they are in offices tryin' to run the givernment instead of on the farm where they ort to be."

Just One Little Bite

Chadwick, Missouri

This is little Bobby Dixon and his pup, of Christian County, Missouri.

After wrestling and tumbling on the rug for a while, Bobby decides to take a bite.

The pup, however, doesn't seem to think it's just the thing to do. The artist paused at this tense moment to see just what's going to happen.

Charley Coleman

Yancy's Mill, Missouri

CHARLEY SAYS:

"If you've got any horses you want to swap, bring 'em around. I've dealt in 'em all my life an' I can purtnye tell what a nag is, as soon as I glance at it.

"Horse swappin' has allers been a great custom among us fellers in the Ozarks. Sometimes we give one another the dad-burnedest skinnin's you ever see'd.

"I traded fer a mule t'other day an' the nasty ol' pup jumped out of the lot last night an' got away, an' I'm goin' now to look fer 'im. Ye hain't see'd 'im, have ye?

"Ye cain't never tell what a durn mule will do. The dirty ol' long-eared boogers, ye cain't trust 'em. They'll live fer forty years an' be good to ye all that time, jist to git a chance to kick ye, an' kill ye before they die.

"In my swappin' around, I sometimes git a mule that's balky an' won't work nairy bit, an' I don't know of nairy thing in this world that's half as stubborn as a balky mule. Now ye take a balky womern, an' ye can talk 'em out of a lot of things or talk 'em in to a lot of things, but ye cain't reason with a dad-burn mule.

"Most mules air good pullers, but when ye do find one that won't work, he's usually too ornery to put out enough strength to pull the skin off a banana.

"He'll twist around in the harness, stick his ears straight forward, an' throw his nostrils wide open an' blair his eyes till they look like two golf balls stickin' on his face, an' there the sassy ol' judge will jist stand an' never move a peg, an' dare ye to try to make 'im pull.

"All I do when I git one like this is jist treat 'im good, feed 'im well, an' doll 'im all up an' make somethin' good lookin' to swap on, an purty soon some other feller comes along an' wants a good-lookin' mule, an' here's where I separate frum my troubles.

"I'd ruther have a bad case of toothache or the seven-year's itch than a balky mule."

Orville Cassady

The Champion Fiddler of the Ozarks

"I was born on a farm in the hills of Texas County, Missouri, near Houston, Mo. I am of true Irish blood. My grandparents came from Ireland and settled in St. Louis.

"My father was an' ol' time fiddler an' played such tunes as 'Eighth of January,' 'Billy in the Lowlands,' 'Irish Washerwoman,' and the 'Hornpipes,' which were popular in them days, an' it is them same ol' tunes that I love an' cherish.

"To me, this ol' fiddle is not only a musical instrument, I love its ol' tones. It will soothe and content me when everything else fails.

"I have spent many years fiddlin' fer the ol' Ozark square dances, playin' the same ol' tunes my father used to play, beginnin' early in the evening to play fer the dance and keep it up until the rooster crows the next mornin'.

"Gosh, but it's a lot of fun to see some of the ol' boys come wobblin' in about half shot on this wild mountain whiskey, an' when I make my ol' fiddle scream out on a tune like 'Billy in the Lowlands' or 'Stoney Mountain' they jump higher than a ten-rail fence, clap their heels together, the sweat pops out on 'em an' they dance an' holler till you can hear 'em a mile."

111

The Square Dance

This is a drawing of the old mountain square dance as seen in progress at a place known as "The Spot," deep down in the hills of Dent County, Missouri. It is quite a distance from town, and a place at which the mountaineers gather in from all directions, drink beer, liquor, and dance, from early in the evening until the "ol' gray rooster" crows the next morning.

They are seen here as they dance the well-known figure, "Cheat or swing." The dance started at the scream of the fiddle on the ol' tune "Hell Up Skunk River," when the caller began to clap his hands, stamp his feet, and cry out:

"All to your places,
    and straighten up your faces,
    take up your back-bands,
    and straighten out your traces!

Now you dance, and now you swing,
    and how can you cheat that purty little thing.

Half way round, then turn back, with the lady
    in front and the gent behind,
    and swing 'em around till they go stone-blind!"

This is a very interesting figure, and one that is difficult to understand and dance, as everyone seems to be working hard, jumping high, winding and twisting here and there, but all are enjoying the fun and having a great time, in the old-fashioned way.

The square dance has always been the most popular amusement for social gatherings among hill folks, and is frequently held in private homes far back in the hills, where pie suppers or box suppers are held in connection with the dance. The lady of the house wherever the dance may be, will have a number of pies baked—if it happens to be a pie supper— or if a box supper, the girls from the neighborhood will cook up chicken, pumpkin pies, cookies, etc., fill their boxes, with their names written on cards and placed within, and take them along, and after they have danced until around midnight, and all are hot and hungry, then the pies, or boxes, are put up and sold at auction to the highest bidder, after which the boys and girls go away in couples and have supper; then the dance starts again and goes on until daybreak.

The fiddler usually gets free lunch and free drinks, but the first thing of all is to give the "fiddler a dram," and this is done by the good-natured old boy, who, dressed in overalls an' coarse shoes, comes riding his pony and saddle up from way down in the holler with a quart on his hip, leaps from his saddle, ties his pony to a tree, goes in and takes the fiddler out in the dark, and gives him a "snort" of that good old "mountain dew," that enables him to go in, take his seat, cross his legs, and rasp out one after another of the old hill tunes that put the quibble and jitter in the boys and girls, and keep it up untiringly until sunrise the next morning.

Green Hodges

Rector, Missouri

MR. HODGES SAYS:

"I am eighty-one years old and a native of Howell County, Missouri. I am an old Ozark deer killer and have lived here all my life.

"I don't guess there's any doubt that I have killed more deer than any man that ever roamed these hills. I've killed about 250 with this old muzzle loader you see here.

"When I was growin' up from boyhood, I have seen times so hard that we had nothin' to eat and had to hunt for a livin'. I have walked miles and miles and miles, through deep snows trailin' deer up to kill.

"I have seen the time when they was so numerous that they would git into our fields and eat up our corn and beans. It was no trouble to kill 'em then, and I have killed as many as four and five in a day.

"About the best way I've ever found to kill deer is to make what we old hunters call a 'deer lick' and we do this by goin' out on some high place or main divide where deer cross over from one holler to another, an' there we put out salt for 'em to lick. We then build us a scaffold in a tree about thirty feet high and about one hundred yards from the lick, and sit on that scaffold in the nightime and kill 'em as they come up to lick salt.

"By settin' real quiet, you can hear 'em trampin' through the leaves from all sides as they come up from the heads of deep hollers around the lick.

"Their eyes shine like balls of fire and that's what we see and shoot at. We can't see the deer in the darkness, just their shiny eyes, and we can shore get 'em.

"From about ten o'clock to twelve in the night is the best time to kill 'em. I have allers kept a good dog and gun, and have found it purty easy to make a livin' in the Ozark hills. Us fellers used to git together and take our dogs and guns and go out on a big deer drive, camp out, and have the dad-burnedest time you ever see'd.

"As soon as my dog sees me take my gun from the rack, he begins to fuss and jump and raise thunder to go, and By-grabs, he's really a whirlwind, too, when it comes to huntin'."

Ed Loutherage

Crawford County, Missouri

"I am an ol' Ozark hunter. I'll bet I've killed more turkeys than any other man that ever see'd these hills. Why, gosh-durn, hit's a sight of turkeys I have killed in my life. To tell you the truth, I hain't done much of anything in my life only prowl through these hills with my gun in my hand.

"I killed twenty-six gobblers in the spring of 1907. I made me a turkey caller that just sounds like a hen turkey, and when I lay down behind a log and give that a few yelps, the ol' gobbler comes walkin' up with his neck stretched to see what it's all about and that's when I get 'im.

"In the spring of the year is the best time to turkey hunt. That's when they mate and the ol' hen is nestin' and layin' her eggs to raise her brood. It's plum easy to call the ol' gobbler up then, 'cause they'll come to any kind of noise that sounds like a hen turkey. So when I lay down behind a log to call 'em, I kiver myself up in leaves, all but my eyes and gun, and, boy, I can git 'em.

"I've killed lots of wild ducks, too. One mornin' I went out to a pond where I knowed I'd find some ducks, an' I sneaked up, an' shore 'nough, there they wuz. They see'd me and flew up. I shot into the bunch as they flew away, an' both barrels of my ol' gun went off, an' I killed thirteen ducks. Hit just **rained ducks** fer awile. I never see'd the like."

116

The Lone Fisherman

Oregon County, Missouri

This drawing was made of young Charles Dobson, as he was seen with his dog and fishing tackle (which consisted of a crude sycamore pole, a hook, line, and a can of angle worms), sitting on a ledge rock over a deep blue pool along the banks of the Eleven Point River, in Oregon County.

This youth, with his dog and equipment, has apparently slipped away from the home that's seen far in the background, to have a little sport and recreation all his own, and is seen here in extreme contentment, as he sits in a pigeon-toed position, stringing a worm on his hook for the catch of another perch to add to his number, as the dog looks on, to see just how it's done.

One of the most common scenes in the hill region is the barefoot lad strolling away from his cabin home, along the wild wood's trail, with his shaggy, tattered pants rolled up to his knees, with a can of worms in his hand, a fishing pole on his shoulder, and a hound-dog trailing along behind, as he goes peacefully on his way to the mountain stream in search of a nice deep pool where he may perch himself high up on a rock and fish; or he may be seen slowly wading around in small streams spearing and killing frogs and fish, stringing them on a cord, and carrying them dangling around his neck.

Oregon County is one of Missouri's most rugged counties, and is well known for its high, stony mountains, heavy timber, rushing streams, and large springs.

Along the mountains of the Eleven Point River is the well-known and famous "old Irish wilderness." It is a dense growth of underbrush, and a real harbor for wild game—deer, turkey, wild mountain bobcat, raccoon, opossum, squirrel, quail, and pheasants.

The Eleven Point River is also well known for good fishing, and young Charles, who seems to be taking advantage of the opportunity, says, "Sometimes Ma sends me out after a load ov wood or bucket ov water to cook dinner, and I take my dog and fishin' tackle and sneak away, and go fishin' or frog huntin', and go back to the house with all the fish or frogs I can carry."

Ozark 'Possum Hunters

In Ozark County

This drawing was made of the old torch light 'possum hunters, as they were seen way back up "Possum-Trot Holler" in northeast Ozark County where the hills are steep, high, and rugged.

The pine torch is the lighting method still used by night hunters in the Ozark hills, and has been used all down through the history of hill dwellers. The hunter takes a pocket full of matches, his dog, gun, and ax, and starts away into the hills just at dusk.

The first thing he does upon entering the woods, is to look around to find a nice pine knot, or an old pine snag, that contains lots of pitch, or tar rosin—the correct name—and with his ax he splits this "rich pine," as he calls it, into strips about the size of his finger, and thirty inches in length, and by binding five or six strips together he has a nice torch light that's strong enough to shine on the 'possum in the persimmon tree, or reflect on the 'coon that climbs high up in the tops of the tall oak trees, and while one holds the torch and shines the light on the animal, the other either shoots or knocks it out with a rock, the latter method being the most commonly practiced as shooting the animal sometimes spoils the fur or skin, and if it happens to be a 'coon, the hunter tries especially hard to knock it out of the tree with a stone, in order to see the dog and 'coon battle, which is a great sport, and a thrill to Ozark night hunters.

The hunter says, "It shore takes a dad-burned good dog to whip a 'coon, but I've got one that kin do it, 'cause when I knocked that 'coon out ov the tree last night, him an' ol' Blue fit all over the hillside before ol' Blue killed 'im, but he finally got Mr. 'Coon."

Sometimes the hunter is forced to cut the tree down in order to get the 'coon, as the animal frequently runs into a hole, taking refuge inside its hollow trunk, and in this case, when the 'coon discovers that the tree is falling, he rushes to the outside, and out on a long branch, and leaps high into space. At the instant he strikes the ground, the dog contacts him and the battle starts.

The raccoon has long, sharp teeth, and is a real warrior, and it requires a large, well-trained, and experienced dog to win over this battle king.

If one wishes to hear the story related in detail, then go to the old country store and post office, or to the little county seat town down in the Ozarks where the hill dwellers meet and sit on benches in the courthouse yard, or on the counters in the little grocery store, cross their legs, take out their pocket knives and whittle, swap tobacco, smoke their cob pipes, and tell what a wonderful 'coon dog they have, or how easily "ol' Drum," "ol' Lead," or "ol' Blue," or "ol' Rover" handled and whipped the 'coon last night.

The opossum has no fighting spirit and merely sits humped on a low swinging branch near the ground, where the hunter can knock him off with a rock or club, and immediately upon striking the ground he "sulls," when the hunter picks him up, puts him in a burlap sack that he usually carries along for this purpose, and takes him home alive.

The Squirrel Hunter

Ozark County, Missouri

This squirrel hunter was seen one November morning, deep in the hills of Ozark County, amidst the forest of oak, walnut, and hickory nut trees, where squirrels are abundant, and the roar of the shotgun, and the sound of the "hound-dog's" bark echoes through the hills daily.

The artist saw the hunter just as he was in the act of bringing the squirrel down from the giant oak tree as the dogs eagerly waited to see it fall.

Early morning squirrel hunting is one of the Ozark hunter's greatest sports. He chooses this as the best time of day to find the industrious little animals that emerge just at daybreak from their night's resting place in hollow tree trunks, to have their morning exercise. The hunter sits quietly watching them, with their bushy tails flitting in the air as they play up and down the trees and leap from branch to branch, and do their early morning stunts on twining grapevines, after which they scamper to the tops of tall oak, walnut, or hickory nut trees, to sit and whittle acorns, walnuts, or hickory nuts, and have a good rich breakfast, after which their daily work of carrying and storing away nuts for their winter's supply begins.

The early morning hunter seldom takes his dogs along when going into the woods to shoot squirrels. He does what is known as "still hunt." By standing quietly around among the timber, looking and listening, he is able to see the bushy-tailed tree animals in all their glory as they go through their early morning maneuvers.

The hunter's most thrilling sport is to shoot the squirrel as he runs and plays on the grapevines that twine through the timber, or fire on it as it springs high into the air as it leaps from one treetop to another.

The most ideal time of the year for squirrel hunting is in the fall—September and October—when the acorns, hickory nuts, and walnuts are ripe, and the frisky little animals are busily engaged harvesting and storing their winter's food.

If the hunter happens to enter the woods too late in the morning to see the activity of these little early risers, then his method of locating—if he is "still hunting"—is to sit around very quietly to hear the sound of their sharp-pointed teeth against the hard nutshell as they sit high up in the tree eating their breakfast. This sound can be heard several hundred feet away on quiet mornings, and frequently fragments of nutshells may fall upon the hunter's head when suddenly he looks up to find the squirrel having breakfast in the treetop under which he sits.

This method of hunting is very effective, and gives the hunter wonderful opportunity of studying and learning the habits of the little wild woods' dweller.

Bill Stagner

Phelps County, Missouri

BILL SAYS:

"Well, I think the ol' sayin' is true, 'A dog is a man's best friend.'

"They are an unfailin' friend, an' will stick to you an' foller you up, even after yer wife turns you down, kicks you out, an' won't foller you anywhere.

"This ol' hound is a real true friend of mine, an' sticks to me like good glue. Wherever you see one of us you see us both. We are real pals, an' ever time I set down, he's right on top of me an' jist kivers me up.

"I wuz born in the hills of Phelps County. I am eighty-one years ol' an' have lived here an' rambled through the Ozarks, an' handled houn'-dogs an' studied 'em all my life, an' I think this is the best all-around dog I know of.

"This is the full blood ol' black back, red-bellied pot licker. They are the best fox houn' there is, an a good tree dog, too. They are good dogs for 'coons, 'possums, squirrels, an' all kinds of small game.

"This ol' houn' is mighty watchful around the house an' knows about ever thing that's goin' on, even to what's goin' on in the kitchen, an' ever time my womern's back is turned, he's lickin' a pot or somethin'.

"He can tree squirrels faster'n you can shoot 'em, an' suck eggs faster'n the hens can lay 'em, an' that's why my womern hates him, but it's why I like him. I even feed 'im raw eggs to make 'im long winded, an' a houn' that won't suck eggs hain't go good a-tall, an' I wouldn't have him.

"When this ol' dog gits after a fox, he might as well hunt his hole, for he never knows when to quit.

"Sometimes he's out on a chase fer three days, an' when he comes in his feet are so sore he can hardly walk fer a week."

124

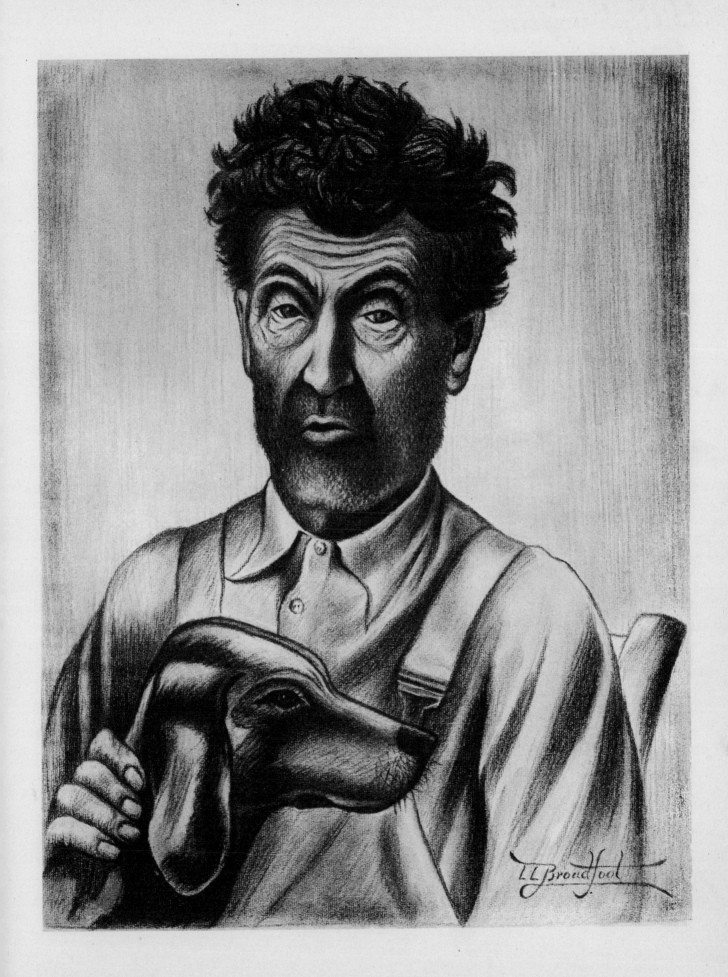

125

Dolph Givins

"I am the Saturday's newsboy. I live six miles frum town an' walk in every Saturday to sell a paper called 'Grit.'

"It's a purty good paper an' I'm a purty good seller. I sell forty-two copies a week at five cents each, an' I get to keep two cents of each five, and shucks, that's better'n nothin'!

"I got a womern an' six 'kids' and by-doggies, it jist keeps us all bobbin' ter make a livin'!

"I get a little WPA once in a while, an' catch a few rabbits, an' do a little of this an' that, an' my womern is a purty good hustler, too. She can plow corn, make rails, build fence, an' cut sprouts, as good as any man. She can shoot a squirrel out of a tree at every shot. And all them things go a long way in helpin' a feller to raise a bunch of 'kids.' "

Mary Rasor

Montauk, Missouri

MARY SAYS:

"It's purty hard work but I love to take my ol' corn knife an' get out in the field in the fall of the year an' cut corn, an' I can shore slice it with this ol' knife.

"Of course, I am seventy-six years old and cain't do so much any more, but I used to, could cut jist as much corn as any man.

"We've got our own workshop, an' make about everything we use—even to the furniture in our house.

"Me an' Nancy can even shoe our horses.

"Bill don't know much, only to make rails an' build fences. We make our corn knives out of ol' worn-out hand saw blades, an' they shore do make good ones, too, 'cause there's real metal in 'em.

"Me an' Nancy an' Bill have allus lived together an' done our own work. We don't hire nothin' done, 'cause we can't find anybody that knows how to do our work like our pappy an' mammy taught us to do it.

"We allers had to work in the fields till the summer's work was done an' the crops laid by, then go to the ol' spinnin' wheel an' loom an' make our clothes.

"Me an' Nancy an' Bill still make about all we eat an' wear, as we did back in the ol' days, an' it takes backbone an' elbow grease to do it, too, but we are not afeard of work, 'cause I don't recon it ever killed anybody.

"We've allers been stout an' husky, 'cause we doctor ourselves by takin' our own medicine that we make out of herbs. If we have anything ailin' us, we go up on the hillside an' dig some roots an' bile it down into a strong tea an' drink it, an' that beats any of this ol' strong doctor's medicine.

"We go barefooted all summer an' fall, an' I believe that's good for us, too. Our feet git a little rusty an' are not so purty, but we don't give a durn.

"It used to be awful wild around here in these brush. It wuz a wild man's country, an' there wuz lots of Indians. People think me an' Bill an' Nancy are Indians, but I don't know.

"The James boys used to hide out around here, an' we have see'd 'em. They stayed all night at my aint's house once, but they warn't bad men a-tall."

L L Broadfoot

129

Bill Rasor

BILL SAYS:

"Nancy an' Mary talk like I don't know how to do nothin' but I can make rails an' build fence, an' here's my 'nigger-head mall an' wedge' that I make 'em with.

"I made this mall an' wedge out of green hickory timber, an' after they wuz made I then put them in the fire an' burned them till they wuz seasoned an' hard, an' by Johnnies, you cain't hardly wear 'em out!

"I made an' fenced this whole place with rails. Of course, Nancy an' Mary helped me. They sawed the timber while I split 'em out, an' they laid the ground chunks an' built up the rails.

"This is what we call the 'ol' worm fence.' They are better than wire fences, or any other.

"When we go to build a rail fence, we allers build on the light of the moon, so the ground chunk will stay on top of the ground an' hold the fence up in good shape. If we lay our ground chunks on the dark of the moon, they sink into the ground, an' rot, an' the fence soon falls down.

"There's a whole lot to learn about how to do things on the farm. Some people don't believe in moon signs, but, by Johnnies, I know there's a lot to it, for I have tried it out.

"People around here call me an' Nancy an' Mary 'ol' foggies,' but, by Johnnies, we don't give a dad-burn, fer we know how to do things an' get along an' make our own livin' without ol' age pensions, WPA, an' this an' that.

"When we come to this place in the early days, hit wuz nothin' but thorn brush an' heavy timber, an' pappy an' mammy died while we wuz young, an' left me an' Nancy an' Mary here to pound out everything we got.

"We never wuz to a movin' picture show in our lives, an' never did see but one nigger. We don't like niggers an' Indians. We only go to town about every twelve or fifteen years."

130

Miss Nancy Ann Rasor

Montauk, Missouri

NANCY ANN SAYS:

"I guess people think that me an' Brother Bill an Sister Mary air funny critters, 'cause we don't go nowhere an' don't know nothin', only stay at home, cut brush, an' run the plow, but somebody has got to throw their back to the sky an' work to feed this ol' world.

"Us three live alone, an' me and Bill hain't never been married neither. Bill is seventy-nine, an' I am seventy-four years ol'.

"Sister Mary married a long time ago, but her man died an' she come back home to live with me an' Bill, an' we jist cain't git along without one another.

"I don't see no sense in this ol' gettin' married. Oh, Godys, none of that stuff fer me! No-sir-ee. Oh, it might be all right to marry, but if I did, me an' my man would jist live together like brother an' sister, cause I shore wouldn't raise no 'kids.'

"I am satisfied to live as I am. No man to kick me in, nor kick me out, an' that's worth somethin'.

"Me an' Bill an' Mary go barefooted all summer an' work like the dickens, but we jist don't like to wear shoes at all, 'cause they hurt our feet.

"You see this horn lying' across my lap? Well, my pappy made it over fifty years ago. It is made of Cedar wood, an' we call it our 'trouble horn.' You ort to hear me blow it. I can play a tune on it. I can play 'Jesus Lover of My Soul.'

"Me an' Mary an' Bill stay at home all the time an' don't harm a critter on earth, nor we don't want no one to harm us, so I've got my neighbors posted that when they hear the sound of this ol' horn, to come. So, when I see a stranger or anybody snoopin' about the place that don't act right, I git out an' give my ol' horn a toot, an' here comes my neighbors.

"I believe in everybody bein' honest an' tendin' to their own business. Some people act like they air so religious when they hain't got no religion at all.

"I think all the religion there is is jist what you do. Oh, of course, I believe a feller ort to fill the 'Ten Commandments,' an' I feel that I have done that, too. I have actually filled 'em plum full, but, of course, I chaw terbacker an' smoke, an' cuss a little, but I guess that's not no bad sin.

"I am a whiskey person in a way. Now if we could all make our own whiskey an' bitters we would all feel better. You cain't get nothin' now, except pizen stuff, without payin' a war pension fer it, an' we hain't got nairy one to pay."

132

133

Luther Boxx

Son of Henry and Vina Boxx,
Hewing Railroad Ties

LUTHER SAYS:

"You can talk about your work an' the different things that you can do, but if you want to really know what manual labor is, jist get in an' swing a twelve-pound broad ax for ten hours, hewin' ol', bumpy, knotty logs with it, an' I'll be dod-gast if you don't feel like eatin' up ever' thing you can get your hands on when you go in at night, like corn bread, beans, taters, cabbage, an' even the petticoat off ov your ol' womern, then I'll treat! Now, boy, you can really lay away the groceries after you hang on to the end ov this ax handle all day!

"I don't reckon there's any work much harder than makin' railroad ties, but I have made 'em ever since I was old enough to lift an ax; an' now I have a fifteen-year-old boy that goes with me to the hills an' makes five an' six ties a day.

"He's never had a chance to go to school yet, 'cause I need 'im to help me so bad. I have a wife an' five 'kids,' an' I don't know what we'd do if we didn't have a little garden, an' get a little relief aid.

"I guess I've made enough railroad ties in my life to lay a string ov track from here to Chicago, an' never got enough money out ov the whole business to buy enough beans an' fat back to last my family twelve months.

"We only git twenty cents a tie, an' we are workin' in timber where the best has been taken out, leavin' nothin' but the old knotty cull trees for us to work into ties; an' I have to work extra hard to make nine a day.

"Well, it's a funny old world, an' it looks like one side was intended to suck the life blood from the other.

"The durned railroad companies could afford to give me a free pass for all my family to ride over the United States, an' give us free meals in their dining cars, an' still be away ahead, for the work I've done for 'em; an' there'd scarcely be a place we could go that we wouldn't run over some ties I've made.

"I've carried my crosscut saw an' ol' broad ax on my shoulder so long I'm humpbacked, an' I've sucked water out of a jug until my mouth looks almost like the muzzle end of a jug, an' still I've never got rich makin' ties."

Thomas Pearl Cawthorn

"The Here and There Man" of the Missouri Ozarks

TOM SAYS:

"I am fifty-four year ol', an' I'm a single man, too. I hain't got no womern an' don't want none.

"I hain't got no address. I jist go here an' there through the hills an' chop wood fer people fer a livin'. I get fifteen cents a load fer cuttin' it, or sixty cents a day. This hand ax is all the tools I use in my work, an' I carry it on my shoulder wherever I go.

"I allers liked to work in the timber, an' don't feel at home anywhere else. If I hain't got nothin' else to do, rather than sit around I take my ax on my shoulder an' prowl through the hills all day long.

"I am out in the hills early an' late. I see the ground hogs sit on high cliff rocks, and chirp. I watch the squirrel as he runs grapevines or sits in tops of tall hickory nut trees an' whittles nuts. I see the chipmunk as he scampers along logs with his pouches filled with acorns an' nuts, storin' them away fer winter's food. I see wild deer leap, an' hear the wild turkey gobble.

"I hear the wolves howl, an' the ol' mountain bobcat as he gives a wicked, vicious roar high up on the brushy mountainside.

"I hear the owls hoot, an' the whippoorwill an' nightingale sing.

"I see an' hear all these things that I love an' enjoy, an' yet people wonder if the meager sum I get fer choppin' wood is all 'Ol' Tom' gets out of life."

136

Mrs. Sarah Tyree

"I am eighty years old. I was born August 21, 1860. I have lived in the Ozark hills all my life. I don't know nothin' about the outside world and I don't care about it.

"These ol' backwoods is a good place to live. We don't try to keep up with styles down here, 'cause style is just what has ruined the world.

"I still blow my coffee and drink it out of the saucer. I am still livin' with the same husband that I married over fifty years ago, but you won't find many these days who will marry and live together that long. They have to try somebody else. People are not nary bit like they used to be. Back when I wuz a girl, people married fer love. Boys would go 'sparkin' on Saturday night and stay all night with the girls. They would help the girls milk the cows, get in the wood and gather eggs, and jist have a good time. When the work was all done and supper was over, we'd set in the kitchen and 'spark' till purty late when sometimes ma would holler out and drive us to bed. But we wuz serious in our love in them days, fer the boys would walk five or six miles in them days jist to see us girls, and would usually make several trips before they 'popped the question'."

139

Joe Wood

Born August 26, 1864

Eminence, Missouri

JOE SAYS:

"Well, I don't reckon that any man ever worked any more nor tried any harder to get along in this world than I have. I am seventy-seven years old and have lived in the Ozark hills all of my life. I have been married twice and have sixteen children, twelve of 'em livin'. I have forty-eight grandchildren an' twenty-seven great grandchildren.

"I was first married when I was only eighteen years old. My present wife is eighteen years younger than I am. I held her in my arms and trotted her on my knee many times when she was a baby, and I thought she was the purtiest baby I ever see'd. When all my children, grandchildren, and great grandchildren all get together, it's railly a big Sunday school.

"I make our livin' in this ol' shop by makin' chairs. I am well known throughout the Ozarks as the 'chair maker.' I make and send them out everywhere. I get $1.25 each for them, an' believe me, they are good and will last. The chair posts and all the rounds are all made on this 'ol' turning lay' that you see here. I operate it by peddling it with my foot. I can make two chairs a day. They are made of white oak timber. My wife helps me and can make a chair about as quick as I can. She used to go to the woods with me and help me saw tie timber. I have made as many as thirty railroad ties in a day, but I finally quit that an' went to makin' chairs, an' now I foller that altogether.

"These are the easiest chairs you ever sat in, and you can't hurt one of 'em no matter how rough you use it. When the framework is put together, I peel the bark from 'lynn trees' and use it to put the bottoms in, and you can see the nice way the bark is braided in makes a good substantial bottom. Sometimes I use white oak timber to make the bottoms, by makin' it into thin splits and braidin' it in.

"A person can find timber in these hills to make most anything they want, an' if the Ozarks hadn't been a good place to make a livin', I never could have raised sixteen 'kids.' "

140

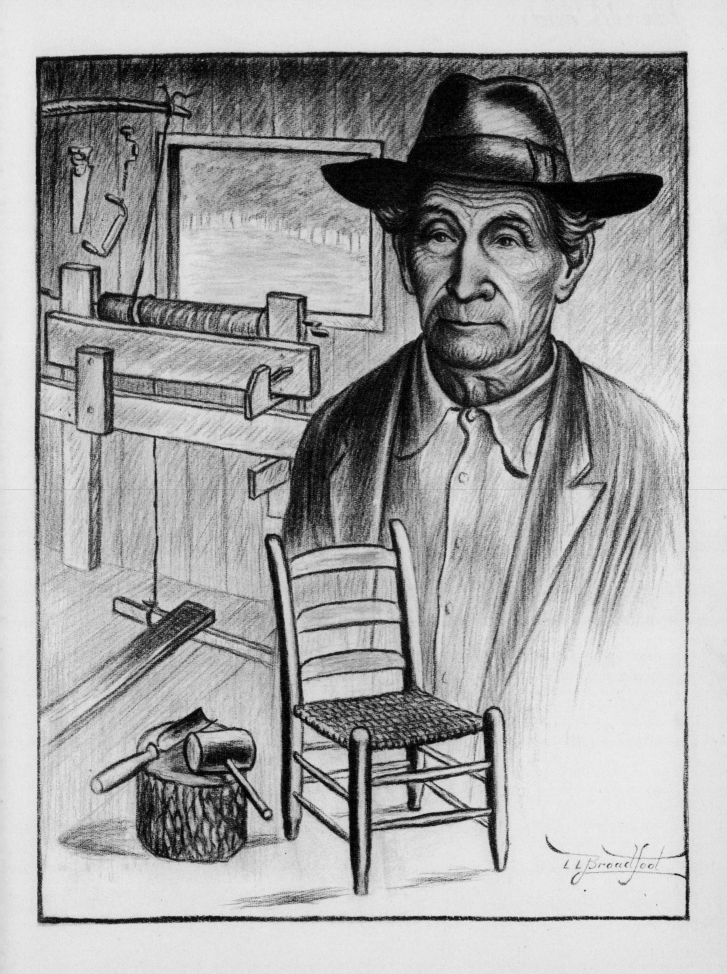

Henry Boxx

The Ozark Board Maker

Elsinore, Butler County, Missouri

MR. BOXX SAYS:

"I am sixty-six years old and a native ov Butler County, an' one of the best Counties in Missouri 'cause we are way off down here in the southeast part ov the state where we have land that will produce the biggest ov anything frum big rivers an' creeks, big timbers, big corn an' pumpkins, big watermelons, big 'possums an' persimmons, big 'coons, big fish an' frogs, an' some purty good-sized snakes an' mosqueeters, but since I've been old enough to work, my job has been makin' clapboards an' nailing 'em on roofs ov Ozark homes.

"I jist wish I knowed how many boards I have made, an' how many Ozark shacks I have kivered in my life. I split the boards out by hand with frow an' hand mallet.

"I made sixty thousand one summer an' nailed 'em all on the roofs myself, besides other work I done. I make 'em out ov white oak, black oak, an' pine timber. White oak, or black oak is the best timber for boards, an' will last longer. If they are made right, an' nailed on the roof right an' at the right time ov the moon, they will last for thirty-five years.

"I allers nail 'em on in the dark ov the moon, an' they lay flat an' make a good smooth roof; but if you nail 'em on in the light ov the moon, that is when the moon is shinnin', then they will curl up at the end, pull the nails frum the lath, an' come loose frum the roof, an' hain't no good at all.

"I am well known all through the Ozark hills as the 'board maker an' roofer,' an' can take you back today to log cabin homes with clapboard roofs that I made twenty-five or thirty years ago, that are still purty good roofs.

"There's a lot to know about how to split boards out to make 'em last, as well as to know how to nail 'em on the roof. There's two ways to split 'em—'bastard fashion,' an' 'timber fashion,' an' if you split 'em 'timber fashion,' they soon cup up an' twist when the hot sun strikes 'em, an' will split open an' the water leaks through; but if they are split 'bastard fashion,' the board will stay straight, flat, an' will not season crack when the sun strikes it, an' will not leak, an' makes a good roof.

"In my workin' around, I've hearn people in the north Ozark counties laff at us fellers in the southeast part ov the hills, an' say we had nothin' but a paradise for snakes an' mosqueeters, an' that it takes three frogs to live a year down here, an' two ov 'em had to be doctors, an' the other a nurse, but let me tell you, I've see'd some fellers in the north part of the Ozarks who were about six feet six inches tall, an' not enough meat on their bones to make a hamburger sandwich, that didn't look so hot; an' if you would size 'em up an' look 'em over, you'd think their mother wuz an angle worm, an' their father a clothes line."

Rose Miller

Mrs. Miller, who lives deep down in the hills of Phelps County, Missouri, in a small log cabin, on her little stony hillside farm surrounded by rugged Ozark mountains, is seventy-two years old, very small in stature, weighing only eighty-seven pounds, but she is extremely energetic, and well known as one who walks everywhere she goes. She was busily engaged in churning buttermilk in her old cedar churn as her picture was being drawn, and when asked how she liked to live in the Ozarks, she replied:

"Well, gee whiz, I don't know nothin' only Ozark life, an' a rugged ol' life at that. Ye jist ort to see the big family I've raised, an' know what all I've had to do to raise 'em. I'll bet I've walked more miles than any other critter on earth. We live seven miles frum town, an' I usually make three trips a week, an' walk the whole round each time, 'cause peepul air so stuck up these days, they won't pick ye up an' give ye a ride. They act like it does 'em good to pass ye by. So I never wuz in a car but jist a few times in my life.

"I walk all through these hills an' dig roots, gather walnuts, hickory nuts, hazelnuts, an' pick berries, an' then walk to town an' peddle 'em out among the merchants an' buy things fer the family.

"Every time I go to town I take a sack ov somethin' on' my back, or a basket ov somethin' on my arm, to sell when I get there, an' buy somethin' to carry home.

"I get up early in the mornin' an' walk out in the hills an' drive my cows in an' milk 'em, an' I have to drive 'em in at night too.

"Pleg-goned if I ever see'd the like! It seems like every thing is piled on me, an' I guess if it hadn't been fer the wild grass that feeds my cows, an' the roots an' nuts an' berries an' things that I gather from the hills, an' the buttermilk that I peddle an' sell frum this ol' cedar churn, we never would have lived.

"I jist wish I knowed how many miles I have walked in my life. But after all, I guess it is lucky for us that we live in the Ozarks, 'cause I don't know of any other place that we could pick a livin' off ov the brush, or live off ov the range."

Ed Lehman

Carter County, Missouri

Ed, who is an explorer, and seeker of hidden treasures in the Ozarks, says:

"I am seventy-six years ol', an' I reckon I've lived under the ground about as much as I've lived on top. I have spent my life since I've been old enough to work, crawlin' in caves all through the Ozark Mountains, lookin' fer gold an' silver, an' money an' other valuables that wuz hid away here by the Indians an' Spaniards before the white race ever settled here.

"Ov course, I hain't never found nothin' yet, but I know it's here, an' I'll find it some ov these days. I've see'd some awful sights under this ol' earth where I crawled back fer hundreds ov feet on my hands an' knees explorin' caves, with a little pine torchlight in my hand.

"There has been times when I wuz scared, an' things looked purty bad when I would come to where the main channel would fork, and I would wind around an' get lost an' have an awful time findin' my way out.

"There has been a good many times when it looked purty dangerous when I would scare up an old mountain wild cat or a wolf, that would run out past me.

"There is thousands and thousands ov bats stickin' to the ceilin' ov these caves, an' they fly all around ye, an' strike ye in the face, an' there's high water falls, an' deep, blue pools ov ice-cold water. There is some of the most beautiful rock formation that one could imagine.

"I go in some caves where there's great flocks ov buzzards. There's lots of people that don't know where the buzzard goes for the winter, but they live in the caves here in the Ozarks all winter long.

"I carry my lunch kit an' hand pick with me wherever I go. I hain't got no home. I stay here an' there among the folks in the hills, an' git my night's lodgin' for cutting a little wood or helpin' to do the chores, an' lots ov times I sleep out.

"I know of a place where forty thousand dollars was hidden by the Indians, an' I'm shore I can find it, an' if I do, I'm goin' to quit crawlin' in caves an' take it easy the rest ov my days.

"I know the Ozark hills inside an' outside, an' I don't know which side is the purtiest, but I have been in some purty close places on the inside, when it looked like I was goin' to have to stay there."

147

Mrs. Lissie Moffitt

Turtle, Missouri

Mrs. Moffitt, who lives alone in her cabin home deep in the Ozark hills near Turtle, Mo., with her chickens, cow, and a "hound-dog" as her only companions, says:

"Well, I reckon you want to know somethin' about my life an' how I've lived, but thair hain't much that I can say, only that I am just another one ov them ol' 'Ozark mothers' that wuz born an' raised here an' don't know nothin' only hill life.

"I am eighty-five years old, an' wuz married when I wuz purty young, an' raised my family of four girls an' they all married off, an' my husband passed away years ago an' left me alone, an' that's the way I live, only at times when I go and stay a few days with my daughters, an' they visit me once in awhile; but I don't ever get lonesome 'cause I got plenty to keep me busy.

"I got a cow an' some chickens, an' a dog, an' I raise my own garden, an' terbacker. I chaw an' smoke, too, an' I jist can't use their ol' sweet, flat terbacker that you buy at the store, 'cause it don't taste right to me. I usually have my terbacker patch up on the hillside back of the house, 'cause I think it grows better an' stronger on a sunny south slope, an' when it matures an' begins to turn yaller, I cut it down an' hang it in the smokehouse till it cures up, then I make it into twists, an' hang it on the walls in the house, an', say, hit shore is good to chaw an' smoke then!

"Hit's mighty nice to have all these things that you've raised yourself, an' can sit an' spit in yer own fireplace in the wintertime when the ground is all kivered with snow, an' enjoy life. I pick an' can enough wild berries every summer to do me through the winter. I take my basket on my arm an' go out into the hills an' stay all day, pickin' huckleberries an' blackberries.

"I keep a dog to mind the varments off my chickens, an' he shore does a good job ov it, too. He often wakes me up at night barkin', an' I go out an' he'll have a 'possum up a tree in my yard, an' I knock it out with a club an' he kills it.

"We've got lots ov 'possums an' foxes, wildcats, weasels, an' hoot owls here in these hills, an' they air all bad after chickens, an' if I didn' keep a dog, I couldn't raise chickens. Once in a while an' ol' hen wakes me up in the night squallin' an' I jerk my clothes on an' run out—an' my ol' dog always gets there first—an' we usually find a weasel or a 'possum in the hen house, an' my dog grabs an' shakes him like a rag, but sometimes they kill a few chickens before I get there.

"I don't know about the rest ov the world, but I hope everybody is as happy and contented as I have been all my life."

L.L. Broadfoot

The Old Log Shop

This quaint old shop setting, which is typical of Ozark hill life, and around which is strewn junk iron of various kinds—old wagon hubs, worn-out wagon tires, discarded wheat cradles, wooden plows, brush hooks, hand adds and hoes—and various other discarded relics, indicating that it has been a place of service and a workshop for Ozarkians for ages gone by, is located on a farm owned and operated by W. J. Randolph on the banks of the beautiful and rugged Current River fourteen miles north of Eminence, Missouri.

Mr. Randolph, who is now eighty-eight years of age, has resided here for sixty years, and, being a splendid blacksmith, a carpenter, and genius himself, has rendered years of service to neighbors and Ozark friends, who come from miles around to the old log shop where they make their wooden hand plows, reap hook handles, harrows, wagon tongues, spokes, and hubs, and refill, and retire wagon wheels; and even make old wooden dining tables, bedsteads, and wooden churns, that are used in their homes.

At the age of eighty-eight, Mr. Randolph does not feel able to work in the shop any more, but is very neighborly and kind-hearted, and still permits neighbors and friends to come in and make use of this old log structure that was built back in the Civil War days.

The farm on which this shop stands has been in cultivation about 105 years, dating back to 1836, and is beautifully situated along the bend of the river, in the low fertile valley where the water makes a long sweeping curve running southwest to where it strikes the mountain of high cliffs and heavy timber, changing the stream to a southeasterly direction. All along the valley, the bur oak and sycamore trees are tall and massive.

One either side of the valley there's a chain of winding lofty mountains covered with oak, pine, and cedar timber. On the west side of this farm, and high up on a mound seemingly planned by nature for the purpose of a home, stands the tall ten-room frame house overlooking the beautiful winding river of rushing waters, with the snow-white branches of the tall sycamore trees contrasting against backgrounds of dense, dark green foliage. From the doorway of this old farm home, one is able to view one of nature's greatest displays of Ozark beauty.

Standing upon a knoll, about four hundred feet from this old log shop, is a giant white oak tree, the top of which is broad and massive, and the trunk of which is about five feet in diameter, very knotty, gnarled, and rugged, around which the Indians used to camp, and where many Indian relics have been found.

This tree was also used for pressing fur, or skins of animals, back in the Civil War days, by an old storekeeper, named "Killis Deatherage," who lived on this farm at that time, and kept a stock of goods in an old log house, only a few hundred feet from this tree, and near by the log shop. A notch was cut in the trunk of the tree near the ground, and by placing one end of a pole or stick of timber in this notch, and pressing down at the free end, the storekeeper was able to bale the skins together in a package, all ready to haul to St. Louis, where he traded fur and animal skins for goods for his store. The hauling was done with oxen, and it required six weeks to make the trip.

Whiskey was also sold from this old storehouse, but it was made by the mountaineers near by.

150

151

Richard Shiffler

Salem, Missouri

MR. SHIFFLER SAYS:

"I am ninety-four years old and a carriage maker by trade.

"I was born July 7, 1847, and took up the blacksmith trade as soon as I was old enough to work, and became a carriage maker.

"I made all my own tools that I used in my work. I made money and done fine, until these durned old automobiles come in, robbed me of my profession, and drove me out of business, and I had to lay my tools down and walk out.

"It's a durn shame! If anyone would have told me forty years ago that there would be somethin' invented to take the place of the purty carriages I made, I would have called 'em crazy. I made the fancy high-priced kind, and saved up some money, and it makes me mad every time I look at a durned old car.

"They are the very thing that has bankrupted the world and put people on the bum. They are just a fast streak of waste and extravagance that has caused all the world to go speed crazy and do nothing but burn up time and money.

"I hate to hear the name of a nasty old car mentioned. It would be good for everybody if they had to come down a notch and set their cans on the old carriage seat once more.

"What a nasty mess of monkey business they have got this world into!

"People will come in from their work in the evening with plans for a hundred-mile trip after supper, to burn up their day's wages, and when pay day comes, they hain't even got enough money to make the next payment on the car they are flyin' around in.

"If they had to make the trip in the old carriage that's pulled by horses or mules, they wouldn't plan so many trips.

"But, there you go! and where are we goin' to wind up?"

152

153

Ed Hoagland

Texas County, Missouri

ED SAYS:

"I have had a lot of experience in my life and done a lot of different kinds of work, an' we never know what we'll be doin' in the windup, or what our occupations will be.

"I am seventy-four years old, an' have seen some very thrillin' an' wild times in my life. I went out West when I wuz a young chap, an' began a cowboy career an' rode the Western range for forty-three years, hurdin' cattle an' sheep.

"I have rode from the Canadian border to the Gulf of Mexico. I worked an' rode the range for Kit Carson for four years. I knowed ol' Kit like a book, an' saw some of the scarriest times of my life while with the ol' boy.

"I used to go up and down the West breakin' an' ridin' wild horses for ranchmen. I used to buy horses through the states of Montana, Wyoming, North and South Dakota, and drive 'em through to southern Texas an' Old Mexico, an sell 'em.

"I have slept out on the prairie among the cactus with the coyotes howlin' around me, an' the rattlesnake crawlin' across my legs. I have been caught out in them northwestern blizzards and almost frozen to death, an' covered up in snow a many a time.

"And now after all this experience, I finally come back to the Ozark hills, an' my present occupation is cleanin' hen houses, and killin' rats. I make my livin' with these six rat terrier dogs by goin' from home to home, through these hills, cleanin' out people's hen houses an' killin' the rats.

"I dig the rats from their dens with a small hand pick an' the dogs catch 'em and kill 'em. Here is ten rats that I killed in about five minutes. I get five cents a rat. I live alone with nothin' to care for but these six dogs.

"It's a funny way to make a livin' but I'm doin' it, and if you want your place ridded of rats, we can shore do the job."

154

155

Oliver Olcott Woodland

Ozark Stone Mason and Monument Maker

Salem, Missouri

MR. WOODLAND SAYS:

"I am seventy-five years old and a native of Pulaski County, Mo. I am a stone mason and monument maker by trade. As far back as I can remember in my childhood days it was my ambition to become a great stone mechanic.

"When I was a young lad, I worked in the timber making railroad ties, hewing them out by hand, with the ol' broadax. This was not the kind of work that I was interested in, but I had to do it for a while to help provide a living for the family, but I soon broke away and took up stone masonry, with no one to train me or show me what to do.

"The first thing I did was to establish a small workshop, which was very quaintly furnished—just a stone pick, a small hatchet or stone ax, a wooden hand mallet, and a chisel. At this point I began my life's work.

"I was rather young, and my first masonry was building chimneys. I have built stone chimneys to many Ozark log cabin homes.

"I get my material by going high into the hills on the main divides, and there I find ledges and cliffs of lime rock, and sandstone, and with my stone pick, and stone ax, I am able to cut this rock out in thin sheets to the desired size.

"It is splendid material for making chimneys, using large flat sheets for arch rocks, hearthstones, and jam rocks for the fireplace. I take it into my workshop and there I dress it down, making it into gravestones and monuments.

"My work is well known and has a wide distribution. I have spent most of my life doing this only. And by visiting the little cemeteries nestled back upon the hills in the Missouri Ozarks, amidst the wild forest, one will find many of them dotted with gravestones and monuments that I have made in my little workshop. There amidst wild flowers and beneath robes of wild roses will be seen the little handmade tomb from Ozark Mountain stone bearing inscriptions and scrolled ornaments which I have made with hand mallet and chisel long ago.

"Looking down from high Ozark Mountain peaks into the rugged valleys amidst dense forests of giant oak and maple trees, one is able to see from the old log cabin homes blue wood smoke rising from stone chimneys that I built years and years ago."

157

Hardin Pace

HARDIN SAYS:

"I recon the Ozark peepul air the funniest critters on earth, an' about the most independent an' self-reliant peepul you ever see'd.

"When you begin to quizz 'em to find out what they know an' what they can do, you'll find out that the average Ozarkian is purty dod-gasted smart, an' can do a whole lot of things.

"We purtnye have to be able to do a little of this, an' a little of that, an' so an' so, to be able to muster up a livin' in these ol' stony hills. I know I have done a lot of different things, an' I'll bet you a 'coon skin that I've got a record that thair hain't many other fellers got.

"I have been a preacher, a photographer, I've been married six times, an' killed three hawks at one shot.

"I first started out to preach fer a livin', but, gee whizz, I soon see'd that that warn't goin' to git me nowhere, 'cause all I ever got out of it wuz maybe a night's lodgin' with some ol' brother who fed me on corn bread an' gravy. I hardly ever got or even see'd a chicken leg.

"Next, I started out to be a 'picture man.' I bought me a camera an' begin to makin' the ol' tintype pictures. Well, this wuz purty interestin' an' I learn't a whole lot about it, but shucks! they warn't even no money in that, 'cause many times when I took a picture an' got it all finished an' delivered they wouldn't have no money to pay fer it, an' I'd have to take a poke of dried apples, or a few twists of terbacker or somethin', to git my pay.

"Well, I quit this dad-blamed no-pay job, an' went to gittin' married. I stuck to this an' follered it till I was married six times.

"My first marriage wuz a flop, the second one a flop, the third one a flop, an' I married my fourth wife, standin' on a goods' box in a dry goods store in Salem, Missouri, while the preacher said the ceremony, an' after the ceremony the young folks picked us up an' carried us on their shoulders around the courthouse square, then charivaried us, an' this wuz a flop, an' so on down, till I've had six matrimonial flops, an' it begin to look like, here at the age of seventy-four, that I wuz gittin' marred up in the women business so dad-blamed deep, that all Jehoviah couldn't pull me out, so I have decided to call the dogs off, an' call it a bad job, at least, fer a while, an' now I am livin' alone an' drawin' the ol' age pension.

"Oh, I wouldn't mind to have another women if she's a good one, fer I still think they air the best piece of property a man can have around the place, if things go right."

159

Ellen Boxx

Daughter-in-law of Henry and Vina

ELLEN SAYS:

"All the rest of the Boxx family have been showin' you and tellin' you what they could do, and now it comes my turn to show you what I do to help raise our family of four 'kids.' My husband, Jake, works around sawmills where they manufacture lumber, or at anything else he can get to do, while I go around here and there gatherin' up rags of one kind and another, and makin' 'em into hook rugs an' sellin' an' trade 'em for food and clothes for the family.

"The sort of material I use is old worn-out overalls, shirts, underwear, stockings, scarfs, and all kinds of waste clothin' that people have throwed away; and I set up late at night and cut 'em into narrow strings and sew 'em together, and with this little hook you see in my hand I knit the rug, and here's one I'm jist finishin'.

"I go out in the hills and study the birds and animals, and do the best I can in drawin' out their pictures on my rugs, then with different kinds of beautifully colored threads I work them into the rugs.

"I sit on my doorstep and study the blue jay, the robin, the red bird, the nightingale, and numerous other Ozark birds that come and sit upon my picket fence and sing their songs; and I study the chipmunk as he scampers along my fence and perches himself upon a picket and chirps at me, and also the big bushy tail red squirrel as he hops from branch to branch in the big oak trees that shade our little box house. I study them carefully and work them as artistically as I can into my rugs that you will find in many Ozark cabin homes.

"Me and my sister-in-law, Ethel, both do woodcraft work, and have got a great collection of all kinds of trinkets on hand that we've made—toys of all kinds.

"I have even made all the furniture I have in my house—bedsteads, chairs, clothes chests, flour chest—and every bit of my furniture is my own handmade stuff."

John Wilkins

Ozark Bee Hunter and Dealer in Dogs and Guns

Iron County, Missouri

JOHN SAYS:

"If a feller is able to do different kinds of work, or has different trades or professions as he goes through life, then he can allers have somethin' to do to get by on, an' make a livin'.

"Now take myself, for instance. I am a bee hunter, an' a dealer in guns an' dogs, an' you know, I've got a job all the year round.

"I hunt bees in the summertime, an' in the fall I begin takin' my ol' rusty guns down frum the rack, an' clean 'em up, an' go out an' look fer some feller who's got a worthless ol' dog that he wants to trade fer a gun, or a pocketknife or somethin', an' soon I find 'im, an' here's where I'll trade an ol' gun that you couldn't hit the side ov a barn with fer an ol' long-yeared pot licker that's too ornery to bark or holler if you stepped on his tail; an' I'll take this ol' dog, an' train 'im up to bark an' run rabbits, tree a few squirrels an' things like that, an' soon some city slicker comes down in the woods to stay a few days an' fish an' hunt, an' the first thing they do is look fer a feller who's got a good dog to sell, an' ov course, I've allers got jist the one they want, 'cause I keep 'em trained up to do about everything but dig worms an' go fishin'—so here's where I git rid ov my pot licker fer a good price ov anywhere frum fifteen to fifty dollars.

"Then, on the other hand, maybe I'll have an ol' dog that's too blasted lazy to scratch, even when he's got the mange, an' I cain't larn 'im nairy dad-blamed thing, an' I'll fatten 'im up an' make his hair look glossy, an' brag on 'im a little, an' trade 'im fer a good gun that I sell fer a purty good price. So I trade guns fer dogs, and dogs fer guns, but I allers have at least three dogs on hand to keep. I keep a 'coon dog, a squirrel dog, an' a hog dog. A hog dog is one that's got nerve enough to catch a wild hog in the woods an' hold 'im till ye get to 'im.

"I start my bee hunt early in the spring, an' keep it up all summer. Ye know, these woods is full ov wild honey bees, an' I've got the trick that gets 'em. I first go way back in the hills to where I find 'em suckin' on wild flowers, or suckin' water at a mountain stream or mud puddle, an' thair's where I set down an' watch 'em till they rise up an' fly away, an' I notice the direction they go, an' I foller up in that same direction for quite a distance an' put out some bait—the kind I make myself by mixin' sweet anis an' honey, an' a lot ov other things together—an' here I set down again an' when they light down on this bait an' suck full ov it an' start away, I watch 'em an' foller up till I find where they live, either in a big oak, or a big pine tree, an' thair's where I cut the tree an' get bees', honey'n all.

"I make purty good money at it, 'cause I sell 'em fer one dollar an a half to three dollars a tree, an' I have found as many as two an' three bee trees a day. I have found where they lived in bluffs but I couldn't get 'em out.

"This star you see on my coat is to show that I'm an officer. I am constable ov my township where I live."

L L Broadfoot

163

Tug o' War

Campbell, Missouri

This is Tommy Larue and his woolly shepherd pup, as seen in Tommy's home down in the hills of Douglas County, Missouri, scuffling and playing over the floor. Finally it comes down to what looks to be a game known as "tug o' war," and a contest of strength between Tommy and his pup, with great fun for both.

Mrs. Ethel Boxx

Wife of Luther Boxx

ETHEL SAYS:

"My grandma Mary likes to smoke her pipe and feed her pigs; my father-in-law makes clapboards and covers houses; my mother-in-law gathers up gunny sacks and makes 'em into rugs, scarfs, and things; my husband makes railroad ties; my sister-in-law, Ellen, gathers up rags and make 'em into hook rugs, and I go about all over the neighborhood pickin' up old worn-out men's and women's hats, and make them into baskets and sell 'em and trade 'em for somethin' to eat and wear; and here's one I've jist completed. What do you think about it?

"This is a man's hat that I took and put a block of wood in the crown, then I bent a hickory stick and nailed it to the block, which makes the handle, then I put a mat of shredded paper over the block of wood, which filled the crown to the top, then I placed a cloth over that, and decorated with flowers.

"I took the band from around the crown of the hat, and wound it around the basket handle and tied a nice bowknot, so you see, I have used the old hat and made it into somethin' purty, and you'd be surprised how they sell.

"It's jist an original scheme of another Ozarkian whose tryin' to do somethin' to get by and help raise a big family.

"We have all sorts of tricks and trades down in the hills to get by on, and that's one fine thing about the Ozarks. If one lives here very long, they'll learn to originate and figure out things for themselves, and you'll purtnye have to, if you make a livin' in these old stony hills, and nobody knows that better than the Boxx family does, and that's why we have learned to do this, that, and t'other.

"Me and Ellen even go way back in the hills and gather up pine burrs and fix 'em up and ornament 'em and sell 'em for five cents apiece; and take in several nickels that way that helps us out a lot; and, gee whizz, there's a lot of things a feller can do to get by if they'll only use a little horse sense!"

L L Broadfoot

John Allen

Dents Ford, Missouri

JOHN SAYS:

"I am eighty-two years ol' an' a son of Gilp Allen, the 'crack rifle shot' who fought as a Confederate soldier in the Civil War in the 40th Regiment, Company K, from Illinois, and used this ol' gun.

"He give it to me when I wuz thirteen years ol', an' I have kept it ever since. Now, boys, talk about your good guns an' your marksmanship, but I can take this ol' musket rifle an' knock dead center about every shot. My daddy used it all through the Civil War, an' hit's a sight to hear 'im tell what he's done with it. I recon the ol' musket rifle wuz considered the most accurate gun the givernment used durin' the war, an' this is still a good ol' gun today.

"I'll tell ye jist how good it is. We have shootin' matches down here in the Ozarks, where a bunch of us fellers git together an' rifle off a fat cow, a hog, or turkey, an' each feller pays so much fer so many shots.

"Then we make our targets on boards an' step off a certain number of steps—usually about a hundred yards, an' then the contest begins, an' the feller that does the closest shootin' gits the most meat, an' I'll be dad-blamed if I hain't drove the whole beef away a many a time, an' finally they got to where they wouldn't let me in on the match nor let me have nairy shot with this ol' musket.

"Hit's a winner, an' a 'beef gitter,' but they have barred me out, an' won't let me in on nairy dad-burned match anymore.

"I don't wear glasses even at my age, but when I lay flat on the ground an' peep down through the sights of this ol' gun an' git a bead on somethin', hit'll purtnye be my game.

"I sometimes think that if the givernment had a few hundred thousand soldiers like some of us ol' squirrel shooters in the Ozarks to send across, that we could soon take 'ol' Hitler through a cleanin'. I could trim his mustache 150 yards away with this ol' gun of mine, an' I know fellers here in the hills that could knock 'em off with rocks fifty yards away."

168

L.L. Broadfoot

The Chrisco Water Mill

Sinkin, Missouri

This is a memory picture of an old gristmill that stood on the bank of Barren Fork, a rushing little stream twining its way from northwest to southeast, down through the mountains of north Shannon County, Missouri, where it threw its power into the large undershot water wheel, about two miles from the old homestead where the artist was born.

This mill was owned and operated by W. R. Chrisco and was built long before the Civil War. It continued to do its daily grind of the old-fashioned stone burr corn meal, until only a few years ago, when it was swept from its foundation by the flood waters of this crooked little mountain stream, and was carried away.

Its capacity was quite limited, as its manufacturing process was very slow, requiring about five hours to turn out one hundred pounds of corn meal. The roaring sound of the old mill wheel and stone burrs could be heard day and night in the constant operation of grinding out bread for the hill dwellers who could be seen coming over the mountain trails from all directions, and from miles around, riding donkeys, carrying sacks of corn, with guns strapped to their saddles and hound-dogs following, all prepared to stay overnight and go 'possum or 'coon hunting, or on a fox chase with the old miller, while waiting for their meal.

This was also a gathering place for the mountaineers who met in great numbers, and had shooting matches, swapped horses, guns, dogs, and pocketknives; boxed, wrestled, and ran foot races, and sat under the shade trees around the old mill, telling stories of hunting, fishing, and fox chasing.

These are facts well known to the artist and writer, and are still to be seen and heard throughout the Ozarks today.

L L Broadfoot

171

The Lanham Family

Bunker, Missouri

This is Mrs. Lanham and her four children, of Bunker, Missouri, as they were seen toiling "worrily" up the Ozark Mountain trail on their way to visit Grandpa and Grandma on Saturday evening.

A visit with relatives and friends is looked forward to with keen enthusiasm by the hill folk after their week's toil eking out a living on their scraggy little hill farms.

They like to live within walking distance of each other so they can visit and can attend the community sings. Environment has taken a hand in moulding their attitude, and this has been the custom and practice of the hill dwellers as handed down by the pioneer settlers.

They possess that "neighborly love" of helping each other. They toil happily through the week, with eager thought of being with relatives and friends and neighbors over Saturday and Sunday for a visit, or to go berry picking, nut gathering or camping along the mountain streams to hunt and fish.

Automobiles are rare among the hill dwellers. One mule supplies motive power for farm machinery which usually consists of one primitive plow. This is usually a gentle, kind-hearted mule which all the family can ride, and is often seen on Saturdays conveying the families to their places of recreation and pleasure.

John Hagler

Mr. Hagler, who is seventy-eight years old, is Justice of the Peace of Spring Creek Township, Dent County, Missouri, and is seen here arguing points of law with the prosecuting attorney of Dent County, as he presides in the justice court.

Judge Hagler has been an ordained minister of the gospel for more than forty years, and at the same time he states:

"I am the oldest newspaper columnist in Dent County, having written news articles for the county papers for sixty-one years, during which time I have served as police judge for a term of six years, and was Dent County treasurer for six years."

During his official career, he has become a well-known, outstanding, and prominent figure in Dent County, and in his present capacity as Justice of the Peace, he seems strictly impartial, staunch in his opinion, and unshakable, once his mind is made up.

He states:

"It is my policy at all times to mete out justice to all according to law and evidence, regardless of sex, creed, color, or race, and through my experience in handling cases, I have learned a lot, and have made a study of crime and its cause, and I am thoroughly convinced that the best and most effective way to check crime is through proper home discipline. If children are taught to respect and obey their parents they will also respect and obey the law as they grow up, and are much less likely to enter the courtroom to defend themselves against crime.

"On the other hand, if one is permitted to have his own way—as that seems to be the trend more or less in this day and age—then the law is compelled to make corrections further down the line, which inevitably turns out to the sorrow and regret of all concerned.

"Too many children are turned loose in the alleys these days to get together and plan mischievous deeds, while their parents drive out to roadside taverns, where they can smoke, drink, and dance, and as long as this condition prevails, crime will ever increase."

175

Aunt Matt Maze

One Hundred Years Old

Jadwin, Missouri

Aunt Matt Says:

"Well, I passed the one hundredth milestone of life, the thirteenth day of last October. I wuz born in Monroe County, Tennessee, October 13, 1842. My father owned the Rocky Springs farm near Madisonville.

"We come to Missouri just after the Civil War in company with thirteen kivered wagons, all loaded with men, women, and 'kids.'

"Our wagons wuz pulled by oxen, mules, and horses. There wuz so many kids in them wagons that it wuz just like a big school when we stopped to camp at night and they all got together.

"We wuz about eight weeks comin' through, but we never traveled on Sunday, and allers took one day off in the week to wash and iron our clothes. We shore had a good time.

"I love to travel by land. I heap ruther travel by land than by train.

"Travelers all had to pay toll at every gate to pay fer the roads, an' there wuz a gate every little ways. We allers camped along the creek an' river banks when we could, an' while the women an' 'kids' would fish, the men would hunt 'possums an' 'coon an' shoot squirrels. Then we would all huddle around the campfire, an' fry our fish, an' broil our squirrel on sticks, an' have a good time. It wuz the good ol' days, but I have lived a good long life, an' that's all gone by.

"I still feel good an' in good health. I don't never go to a doctor fer medicine. My daughter, Minnie, is a mighty good nurse; she knows just what I need."

Overton Williams

Lenox, Missouri

"I can take this ol' Colter plow and a yoke of steers, and boys, I'll be dad-burned if I can't tear up the earth! They are the only thing to break new ground with, and I'll bet I've turned a thousand acres with this ol' plow.

"The bar in front of the shovel is the thing that cuts the roots, and the shovel throws them out and rolls up the dirt.

"Us ol' timers have always used 'em, and I don't give a durn how modern they make their machinery, they will never have anything that will come up with this ol' Colter plow to my notion. I can take it and go out in a patch of new ground just after the timber has been cleared off, and just gouge thunder out of things, have all the roots torn out and the patch of land made into a seed bed, and boy, when I get through with it, it railly is fit to plant corn, taters, an' beans in.

"These city fellers will come out and try to tell us fellers on the farm how to do things, but they don't know nothin', and can ask some of the dad-blamedest questions I ever heard.

"Country people hain't half as green in the city as city people are in the country."

Uncle Henry Jones

Eighty-Three Years Old

Texas County, Missouri

UNCLE HENRY SAYS:

"Well, I don't guess there's many of the young people of today that's ever see'd an' ol' wheat cradle or knows what the word means, but here is one that I have had for years, an' have cut thousands of acres of wheat with it.

"It was made by a man named 'Wallace' about 110 years ago. I used to cut my own wheat crop and then cut for my neighbors.

"It used to take two purty good men to keep up with me an' tie the wheat in bundles as fast as I cut it.

"When harvest an' threshin' time comes in the Ozarks, we make a kind of get-to-gether affair of it an' all have a good time.

"The women of the neighborhood all gather at the place where we work, an' kill chickens an' bake pies an' fix up all kinds of good things to eat for the harvest hands. An' when us men come in from the fields all hot an' hungry, let me tell you them long, well-spread tables look good to us. They look like weddin' tables. We don't help one another for money, we jest swap work an' all get along fine.

"The 'kids' all have a lot of fun durin' harvest time by follerin' us cutters an' catchin' young rabbits as they run out into the stubble.

"I am eighty-three years old an' can't swing this ol' cradle any more, but it's still a good cradle an' ready fer use."

Henry Westing

The Saddle Maker of Salem, Missouri

Mr. Westing Says:

"I am ninety-two years old and have made saddles since I was fourteen, so you may know that I've made and sold a bunch of them here in the Ozark hills.

"I make saddles for both men and women, and also make bridles and harnesses.

"I made six sidesaddles for a woman here in the hills one time, who purchased them for her six daughters, and I really didn't expect her to have all the money to pay down for 'em when they were finished, but when she came after 'em she opened her purse and handed me six twenty-dollar bills, and said, 'Now, them six saddles didn't cost me a cent,' and I said, 'Well, how's that?' and she said, 'Well, my husband drove my hogs in from the hills that was raised on the acorns and didn't cost me anything, sold 'em, and gave me the money, and I'm using it to pay for my saddles.'

"Of course, the automobiles have almost robbed me of my trade and put me out of business, but there's still some demand for saddles and harness, but I'm now too old to work at it much any more, though I have done well, and it has been interesting work to me, and my saddles will still be seen on the old Ozark pony's back, for years to come.

"The sidesaddle is seldom used any more but can be seen hanging in the smokehouses and old blacksmith shops all through the Ozarks, veiled in cobweb.

"There's still lots of horseback riders in the Ozarks and always will be, because the hills are so high and rough, vehicles can't be used, so this is why saddles and harness can always be sold here. It is very common, while passing the Ozark home, to see the boy or girl with their pony hitched to a fencepost, saddling it up, to ride far back into the hills to attend a box supper or pie supper at the little community church or schoolhouse.

"I first began my work by making halters, bridles, and whips, then I soon learned to make harnesses, then saddles. I have made hundreds and hundreds of long, lace-leather whips for ox drivers and also cattle dealers who ride their horses through the hills buying up herds of cattle and driving them out to market. Of course, trucks are now used in transporting the stock to the city markets, but horseback riders have to first round them up in the hills and place them where trucks can pick them up; so after all, the old saddle, bridle, and whip, will be used for years hence in the Ozarks."

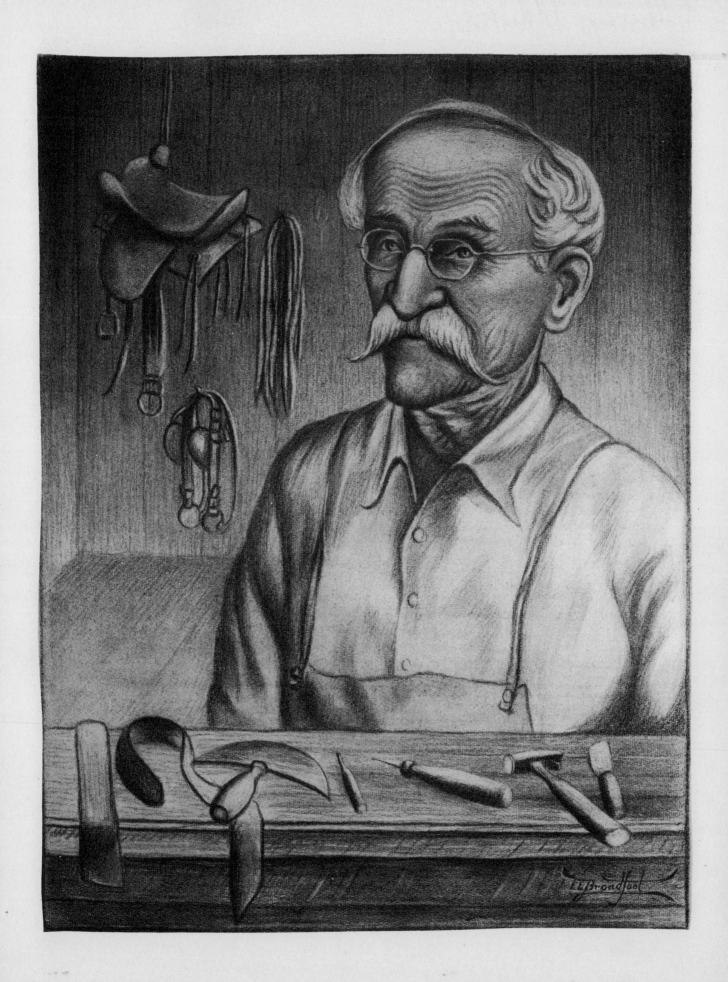

183

Charley Norris

The Ozark Stave Manufacturer

CHARLEY SAYS:

"I am a native of Crawford County, Missouri. I was born and raised near Steelville, and I think old Crawford is one of the greatest counties in Missouri. We have some of the finest water and timber, and some of the biggest and best iron mines in the state, and some of the finest farms and most progressive farmers you'll find anywhere in Missouri.

"I am a timber dealer and stave manufacturer. I started working in the timber when just a small lad, and don't know much about anything but timber. I have been operating sawmills for forty years. When I first began I manufactured lumber and railroad ties, but after following this for a while, I turned my attention to the manufacturing of staves, and for years and years I have had mills sitting on the high peaks of the Ozark Mountains, turning out staves by millions and shipping them to different parts of the United States to be made into barrels for vinegar, pickles, beer, and whiskey.

"I have mills stationed here and there throughout the Ozarks, doing their daily turnout of barrel staves, and nothing gives me greater pleasure than to get up just at daybreak in the summertime and go high up on the mountain peak amidst heavy timber, to look for away and see the smoke rolling from the smokestack of the little stave mill that sits high upon another peak in the distance, or nestled in a deep, rugged canyon below, and hear the chuckle of the engine, and the hum of the big circle saw as she speedily cuts through the giant oak log. It is real music to me, and I often get up and go out early, for this satisfaction alone.

"I often wish I was an artist and could paint the picture as I see and feel it.

"I have worked in the timber for so many years I am not content unless I'm out scanning up and down some big oak tree figuring on the number of staves there might be in this giant old pioneer. And again I wonder just what will happen to the country when all this nice timber is cut away and used up—and that day is coming, unless the government takes the situation in hand and does a lot of reforesting, and the natives are more careful about forest fires. When the day comes that we no longer have timber, then the greatest industry and beauty of our Ozarks will have vanished."

184

O. H. Bryant

Ozark Pen Artist

Licking, Missouri

MR. BRYANT SAYS:

"I am eighty-three years old, and a pen artist of the Ozarks. For years and years I have made my livelihood by going from house to house throughout the Ozark hills, doing pen drawings and scroll work of all kinds, filling out family records, and drawing pictures of birds, flowers, and things in the family Bibles.

"I draw the pictures of turtle doves, quail, redbirds, blue jays, nightingales, and all kinds of Ozark birds, in children's schoolbooks, and with a fine pointed brush I draw them on the walls and windowshades in homes, and even on dishes, and old grandmothers' sunbonnets in inks of various colors.

"Children in the backwoods homes enjoy seeing people come in who are able to do things of this kind, and I find many of them who are keenly talented along this, and other lines of work and culture, and I know that if they could have a little training, they would develop this talent, and become valuable men and women; but since many of them are of poor parents who are unable to send them to school and educate them, this precious 'gift of God' is thrown into the wastebasket and lost forever.

"How wonderful it would be if our government could provide free institutions where poor children could be taken and aided and encouraged along lines in which they are most talented!

"In my going about through the Ozarks, I pick up a few relics now and then. Here is a powder horn that once belonged to Daniel Boone's brother. Here also, is a merchant's account book from Illinois, that's eighty-eight years old, dating back to 1853. I have kept these two relics for many years.

"It is very interesting to read the prices of merchandise in this old book and compare it to prices of today. The articles and prices run as follows: Bacon, 5c a pound; flour, $1.00 per hundred lbs.; lard, 4c a pound; beans, 2c a pound; eggs, 5c per doz.; coal oil, 6c per gal.; sugar, $1.50 per hundred lbs.; whiskey, 10c per qt., or 40c per gal.; gingham, 3c a yd.; tobacco, 10c a plug; gun powder, 10c a lb.; lead, 3c a bar.; gun caps, 10c a box.

"The pages in this old book are very brown, with beautiful handwriting done in ink, with a goosequill pen."

187

H. C. Hammerand

Montauk, Missouri

MR. HAMMERAND SAYS:

"I was born July 9, 1866. I am seventy-five years old. I have lived in this little hut for twenty years. I built it myself from slabs and odd ends of lumber that I carried down the hillside from a sawmill where they manufactured railroad ties.

"I live eighteen miles from town and when I go after my groceries I have the whole round to walk unless someone happens to give me a ride, and that hain't often, and I usually have a big load to carry as I have now.

"People talk about the Ozarks bein' an easy place to live, but I've never found nothin' so easy yet.

"It's a purty place to live, and I guess an easy place to live too, if you don't expect much. One can make a livin'—just an eatible livin'—but you cain't make no money.

"About all the average woods' dweller cares for is a log cabin shelter, a place to sleep, a little corn bread and gravy or sorghum molasses to eat, a gun and some hound-dogs to hunt with, and if they have this and don't owe anybody, they are the happiest people on earth.

"I bought four hundred acres of land in this tract, and built this shack, and have worked hard to try to pay for it, but couldn't, and they took my land back and now I'm just stayin' here.

"I see some of my neighbors who don't seem to do anything only pace up and down the riverbanks, kill crawdads and frogs, shoot squirrels and catch rabbits, that seem to be happy and live better than I do.

"But, that's the way it goes—some can work their toenails off and get nowhere, while others get through easy in some sort of hocus-pocus way and do nothin'."

188

189

Ely Hayes

Gaino, Missouri

ELY SAYS:

"I am seventy-nine years ol' an' hain't never been married yet, an' don't guess I want a womern now, 'cause I'm gettin' too old, an' don't know what I'd do with one. I've been around a whole lot in my life an' see'd lots ov people, but never see'd any womern that I wanted to marry.

"When I wuz young, I worked with the wreckers' crew on the Iron Mountain Railroad, at DeSoto, Missouri, for a while, then I went to St. Louis an' stayed fer a short spell, an' I jist got so gol-durned lonesome I couldn't live there, an' I don't like ol' noisy city life, an' druther live down here in the hills where I can sleep good, get a good fresh breath, an' drink spring water out ov an ol' gourd.

"I've lived alone in this little shack fer forty years, an' every year I plant gourd seeds around my house an' let 'em vine all over this little ol' hut. I like to see these long-necked gourds hangin' on the vines around my porch an' the corners ov my house. The gourd vine makes a fine shade for the house, an' they're awful purty too, an' the gourds are fine an' healthy to drink out ov.

"When I first moved here, I tried to raise corn, but after I had worked hard an' raised it, the wild turkeys would eat it up. I never see'd the like! Why, I've killed as many as five an' six in a single night! An' the deer wuz jist as bad, 'cause they'd jump in the fields an' eat the corn an' beans before it wuz ripe, an' many a time I've sit around an' killed three or four in a day, cut the hams off an' sell 'em, an' leave the rest lie; but I'd like to see you do that today, 'cause if you'd kill a deer now, you'd get your head cut off.

"Some people wonder how I live down in the hills like this all alone, but I'm gettin' along fine.

"I druther live a bachelor's life down in the hills, drink muddy water out ov a gourd, sleep in a holler log, fry me own fritters, an' eat cracklin's, than to take chances on livin' in war like some ov 'em, an' havin' a sack ov beans threshed out over my head or the cook-stove throwed at me, jist 'cause I might happen to say the biscuits wuz a little too hard or the corn bread had a little too much soda in it."

191

The Old Printer

Salem, Missouri

This is a portrait of Mr. Robert Good, editor and owner of the Salem *Post*, Salem, Missouri, who in his old printer's attire—a leather apron, a leather cap, and with sleeves rolled up, and a cob pipe in his mouth—posed for the artist in his printing office in Salem, Missouri, to show the old method of setting type by hand forty years ago.

He states, "I was born in Ohio, but my family went to Nebraska very early in my life, about the year of 1882, where we lived on a farm near Newport. In the year of 1891, just after my father had moved into Lincoln from the farm, I went to Newport, Nebraska, on a visit, where I met an old schoolteacher of mine, who was running a paper.

"Her printer was sick, and she asked me to help her in doing such work as fell to the lot of the devil in the old-time printing office, and, getting the smell of printer's ink on my fingers, I stayed with the job and finally became a printer.

"Following the custom in those days, I went to Chicago and worked for a while, then became what was known as a 'tramp printer,' or what was more euphoniously known as a 'typographical tourist,' and after following this for a few years, working here and there throughout the country, gathering all the experience possible, I established in business for myself, which was about the year of 1896, with the quaint, primitive old set-up of still doing everything by hand, a method used down through the years until finally, step by step, we have come into a perfectly modern setup which has enabled us to turn out the volume of business and give service, through which we have acquired a wide circulation.

"It was the strange coincidence of meeting my old schoolteacher on my visit from Lincoln to Newport, Nebraska, in my early boyhood days, and at which time I had no idea of ever becoming a printer, that led me up to the beginning of my career as a newspaper man."

193

"The Sinks"

"The Sinks" is one of the most beautiful, most popular, and best known places in the Missouri Ozarks. It is situated in north Shannon County, amidst lofty mountains, near the homestead where the artist was born, and was used by the artist and all the neighborhood boys as the "old swimming hole!"

It is a natural tunnel of about four hundred feet in length, through solid rock, about thirty feet wide and forty feet deep, and through which the stream of "Sinkin" flows.

Small boats with passengers pass through. Bathers delight in swimming through, and in plunging from the cliffs into the deep blue pool.

It is noted for good fishing, camping, and outdoor recreation. Thousands go there each year for vacations, and neighborhood friends gather for barbecues, egg and wiener roasts, and Sunday school picnics.

"The Sinks" came into prominence about 1850, when a trapper with gun and dogs, ran a bear into a cave near by, and making a torch from some rich pine splints, he followed his dogs into the cave and shot the bear. Leaning his gun against the wall, the hunter then removed the skin from the bear. He then reached for his gun, and noticed a peculiar looking rock, from which he broke a piece and dropped it into his shot pouch.

When the hunting season was over, he then returned to Tennessee where he had the rock assayed, and found it to be rich in silver. He then returned to Missouri the next season, and the following season, and all about "the Sinks" the hunter searched for the cave where he had killed the bear, but could not locate it. Becoming discouraged, he then gave up the search, and in leaving the camp, he gave the description-of the location of the cave to another man.

Green Carroll, another trapper who was near by and overheard the description, knew the place described, and set out and found the cave the next day. He covered up the entrance, mined the ore, and through some crude process, smelted and ran it into silver dollar moulds. These moulds, it is said, were discarded by the government because of a small crack or flaw in them, and were procured by Carroll through a friend of his who lived in Washington, D. C.

It was this small crack or flaw in the moulds that revealed the money as counterfeit, and cost Carroll his life at the hands of another man who shot him in Tennessee.

The news of Carroll's discovery became so widespread and well known that many men from other states came to Missouri in ramshackle wagons and buggies, loaded with grubstakes and equipment, and camped around "the Sinks," and for weeks and months searched in vain for the lost treasure.

This is a spot in the Ozarks that is well shrouded in mystery, and there is yet to be seen an occasional strange figure creeping mysteriously through the dark shadows of heavy timber, over this stony, lofty mountain bridge of "the Sinks," still searching for the "Lost Silver Mine."

Dr. Abijah Tyrrell, a veteran of the California gold rush of 1849, who lived in St. Louis, Mo., in the early seventies, became interested in the "Carroll discovery," and with several others purchased the land, finally becoming sole owner of "the Sinks" and near-by surroundings. He then moved to the land, built a home near "the Sinks," and practiced medicine among the hill folk for many years. He employed many old settlers of the hills to gather herbs from the mountains, from which he made much of his own medicines, and also, with hand picks, to dig and prospect around the cliffs in search of the entrance to the Carroll Cave.

The Doctor passed to his reward at the age of almost a hundred, and was laid to rest on a hill overlooking "the Sinks," old mining pits, and the early workings for the "Lost Silver Mine."

195